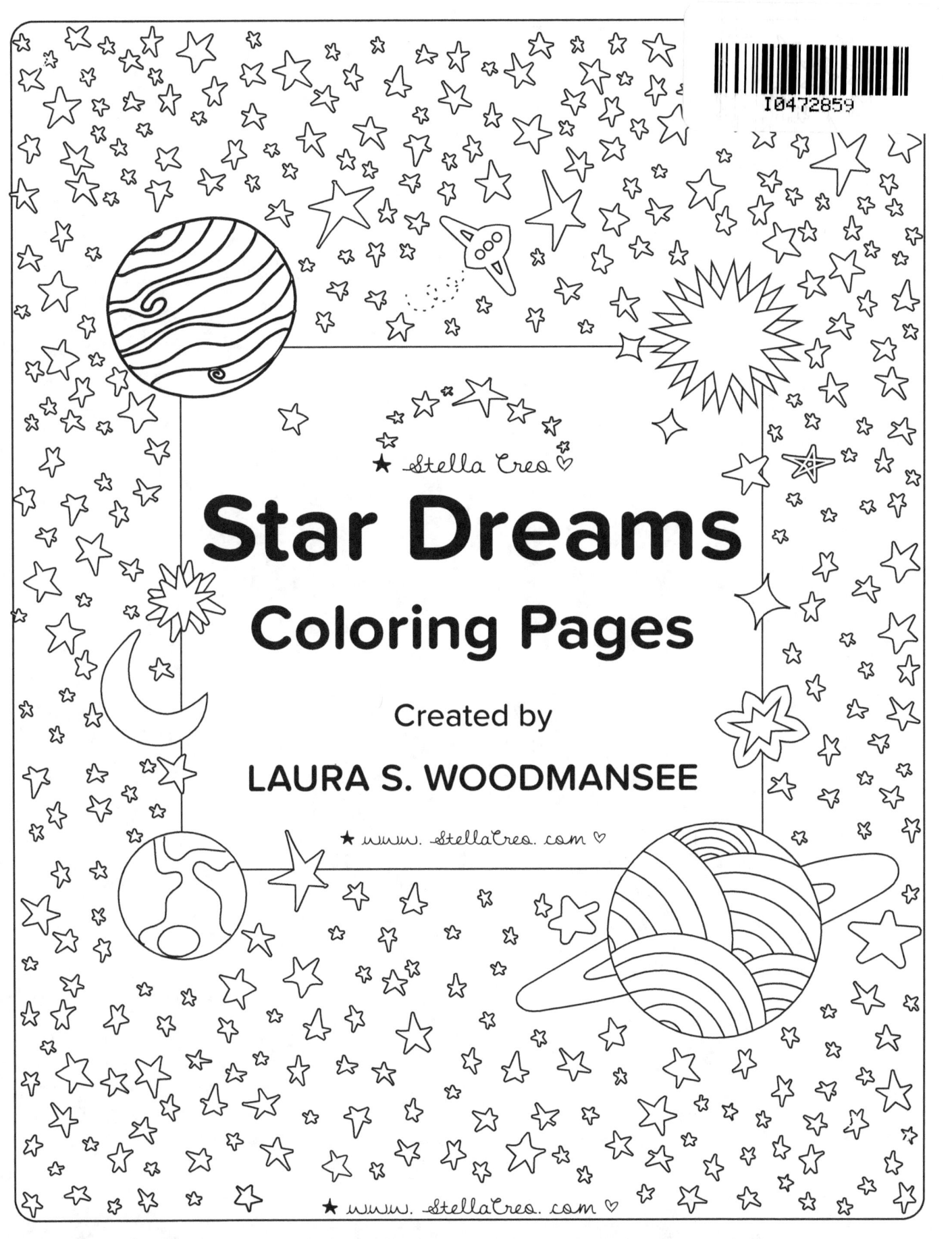

★ Stella Crea ♡

Star Dreams
Coloring Pages

Created by

LAURA S. WOODMANSEE

★ www. StellaCrea. com ♡

★ www. StellaCrea. com ♡

this book belongs to:

www.stellacrea.com

Dedication

For my Readers, Family, & Friends,
Thank you for your loving encouragement.
My wish is that you enjoy this little book
and use it to make your dreams come true!

All My Love,
Laura

STAR DREAMS

Star Dreams: Coloring Pages

Written & Designed by Laura S. Woodmansee

ISBN-10: 0-9863172-3-3
ISBN-13: 978-0-9863172-3-1

Published in 2015 by Stella Creo inc.
Text and Illustrations © 2015 Stella Creo inc.
Stella Creo inc. and all associated logos are trademarks and/or
registered trademarks of Stella Creo inc. www.StellaCreo.com.

Our books are available at special discounts when
purchased in quantity for shops, promotions, fundraising,
educational use, etc. Contact us via www.StellaCreo.com.

Stella Creo inc. creates STEAM-inspired
books, games, and gifts for
kids, teens, and grown-ups too.
www.StellaCreo.com

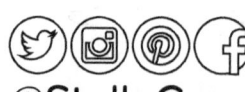

@StellaCreo

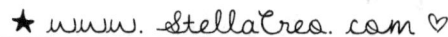
★ www. stellaCreo. com ♡

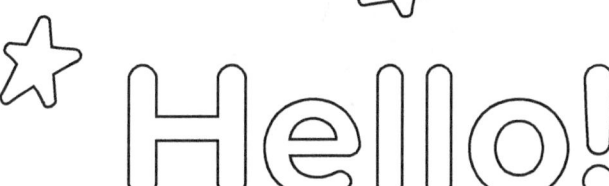

Hello!

Thanks very much for picking up my new book. I created Star Dreams because I love space, star-filled skies, writing, doodling, and coloring!

This project started out as a space-themed coloring book, but I quickly realized that I wanted my little book to be so much more - a place for dreaming, drawing, and planning. When I told my friends, family, and readers, they were really excited! They encouraged me to share all the different types of coloring pages. So, I combined my star-themed coloring pages with space for notes, doodles, ideas, and dreams. I hope that you enjoy the Star Dreams series as much as I've enjoyed creating it all.

This book has two parts; the Coloring Pages section and the Note Pages section. Each has fun, space-themed patterns and designs ready for coloring and creating. The star-themed Coloring section has single-sided pages so that you can use pens and paint that might soak through the pages. I suggest placing a sheet of scrap paper behind the page you are working on. The Note Pages section has space for you to create your own doodles and record your thoughts.

When we take a few minutes each day to create with color we are happier. So, please pick up a rainbow of crayons or markers and color away. The bright, happy colors on white paper will make you smile.

Please share your colorful pages with us on Instagram, we're @StellaCreo. Tag us with the hash tag #coloringbook. We will share too!

Starry Wishes and Happy Creating,
Laura

P.S.: If you like this book, please check out our other Star Dreams series books. The Star Dreams Deluxe Coloring Journal (ISBN 978-0-9863172-4-8) combines this book and the Star Dreams Coloring Calendar (ISBN 978-0-9863172-5-5). www.StellaCreo.com & Amazon.com. Join our e-mail list for free Star Dreams printables and discounts.

@LauraWoodmansee
@StellaCreo

★ *www. StellaCreo. com* ♡

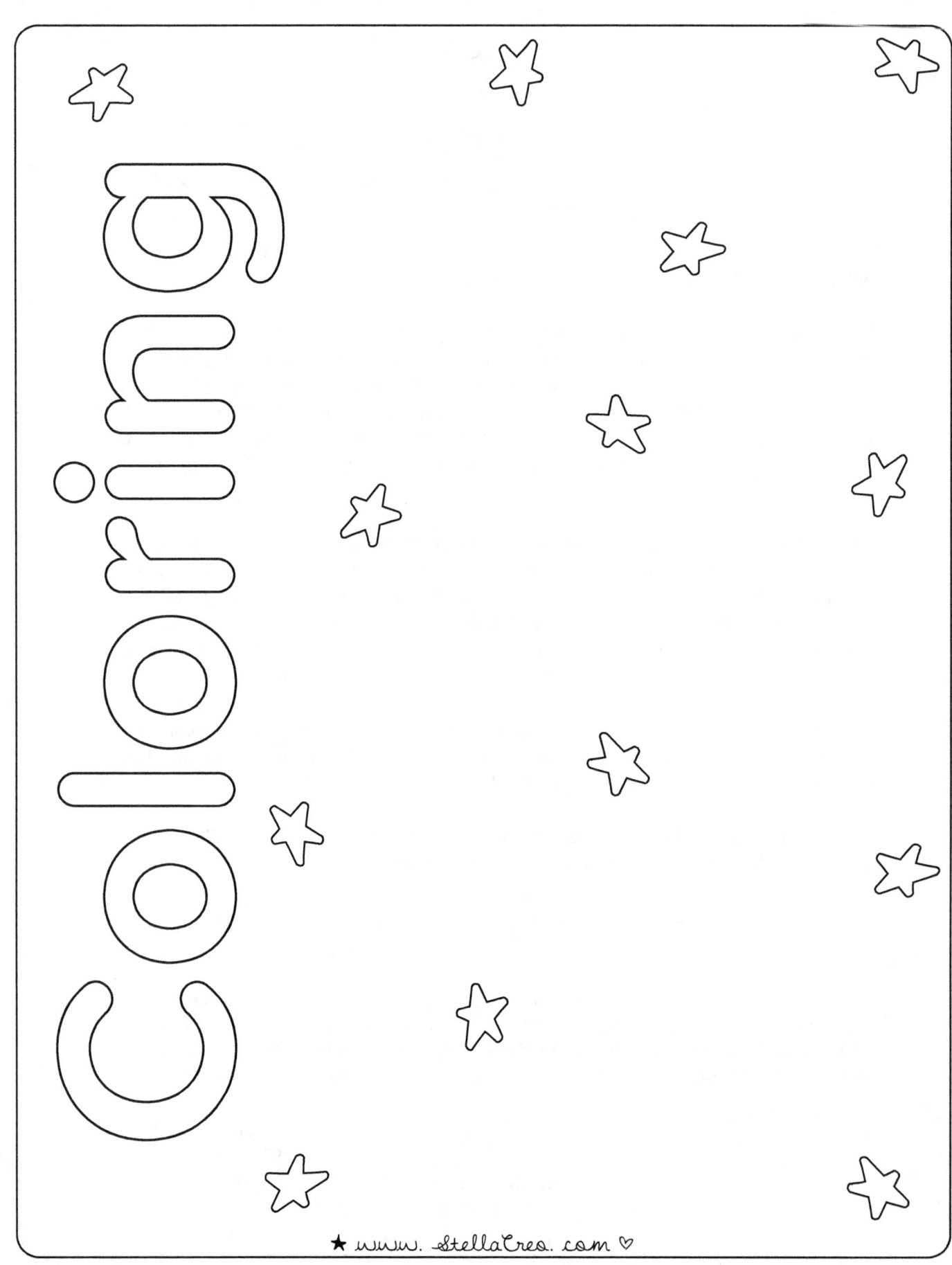

You Are A Brilliant Star

Show off your colors!

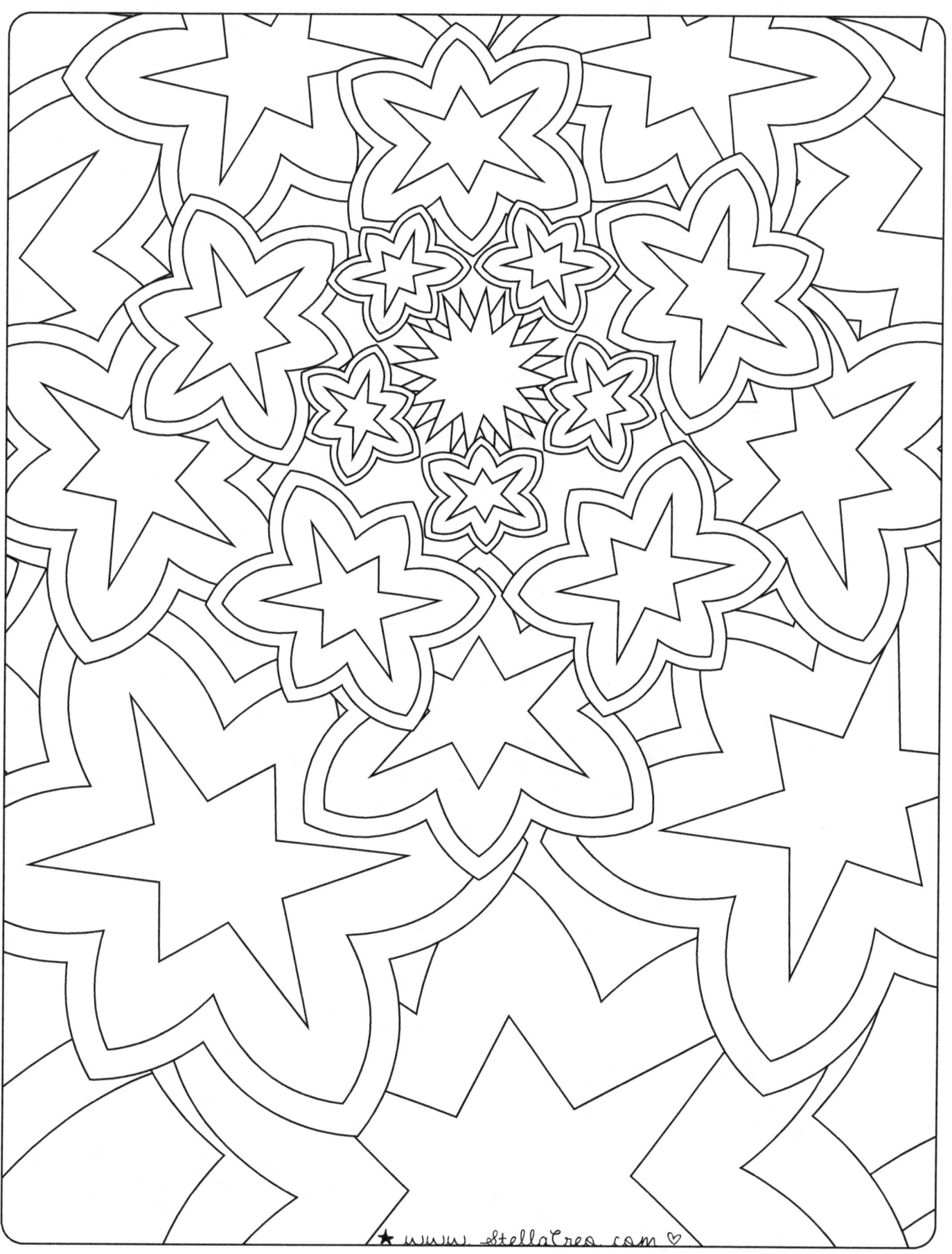

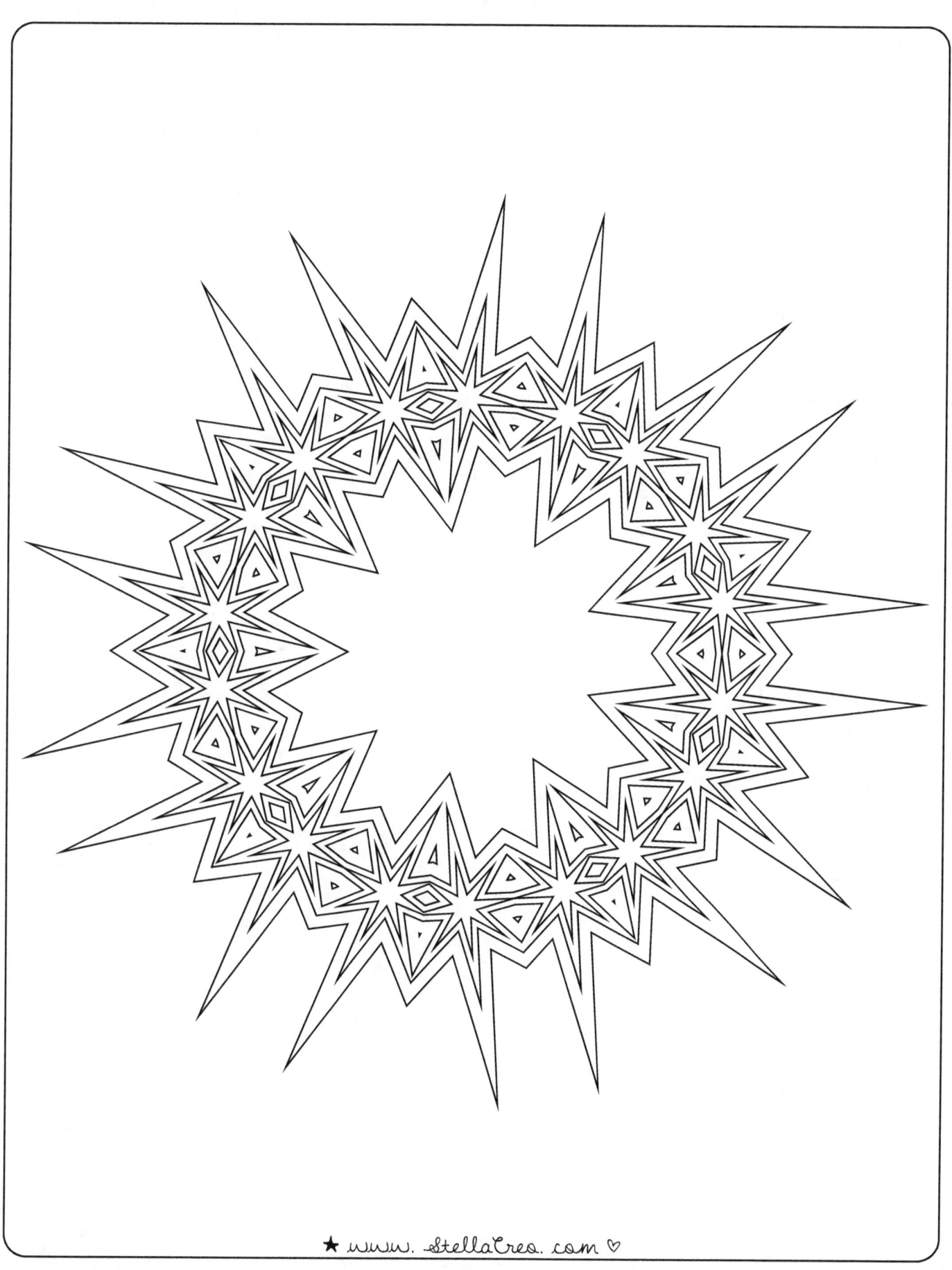

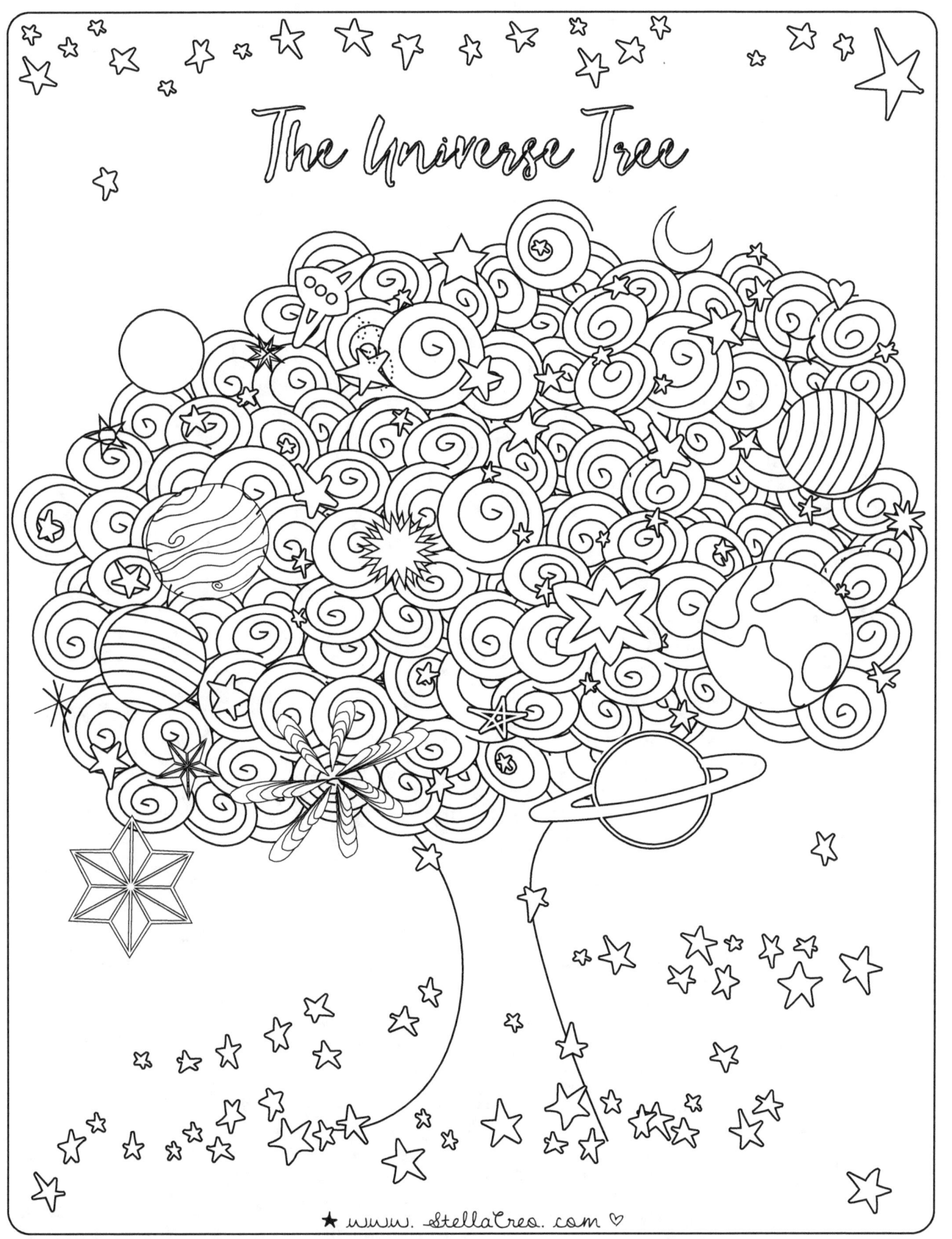

The Universe Tree

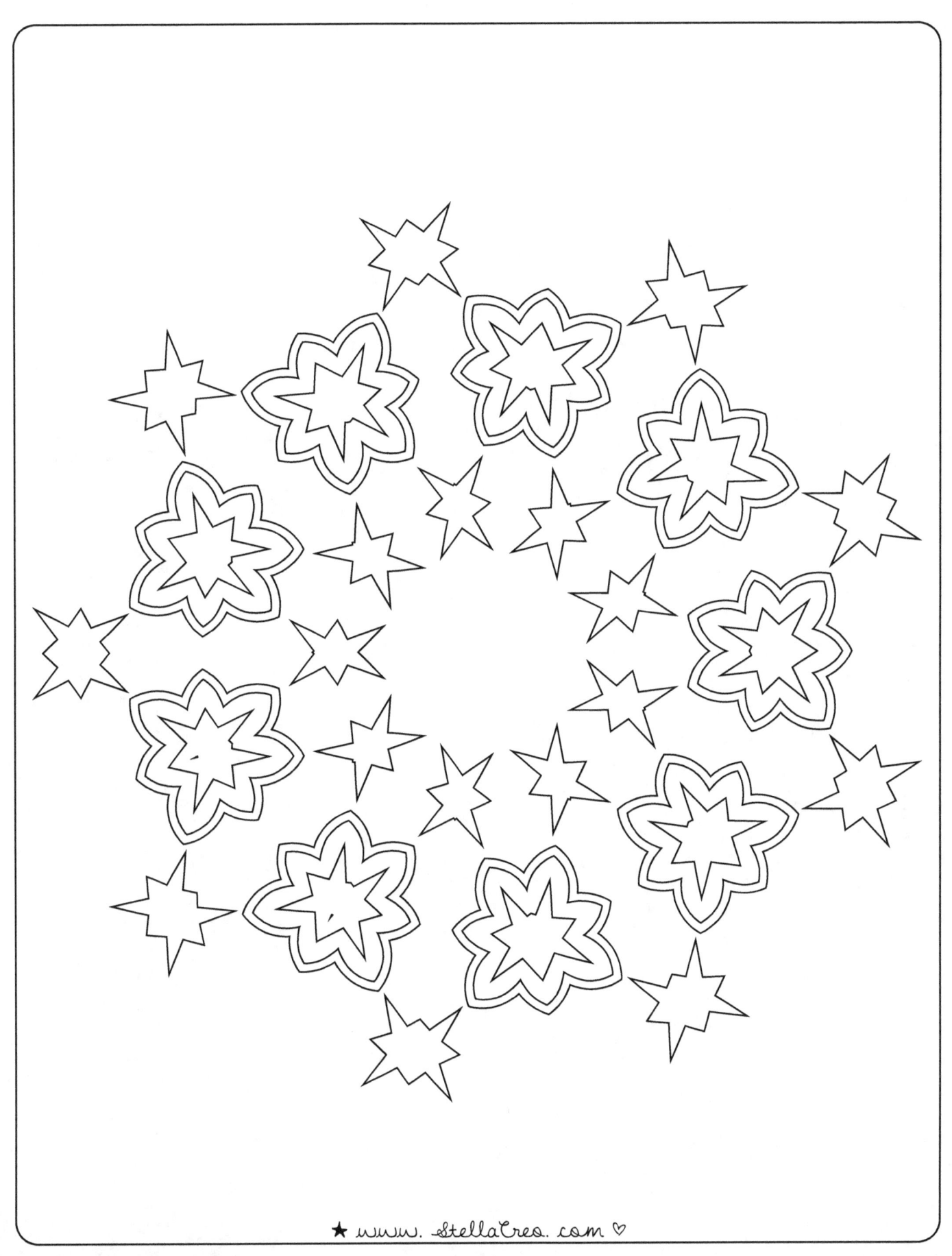

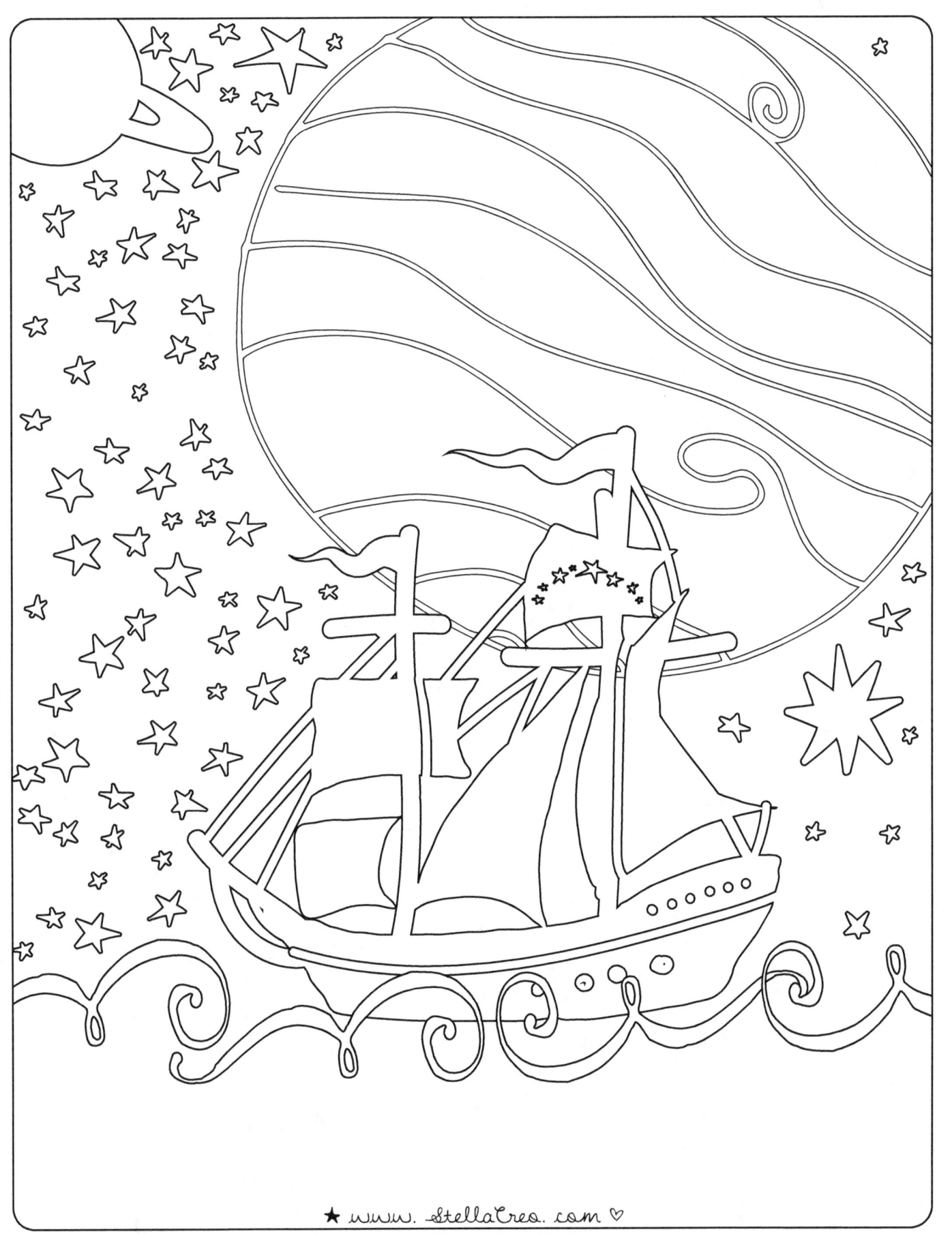

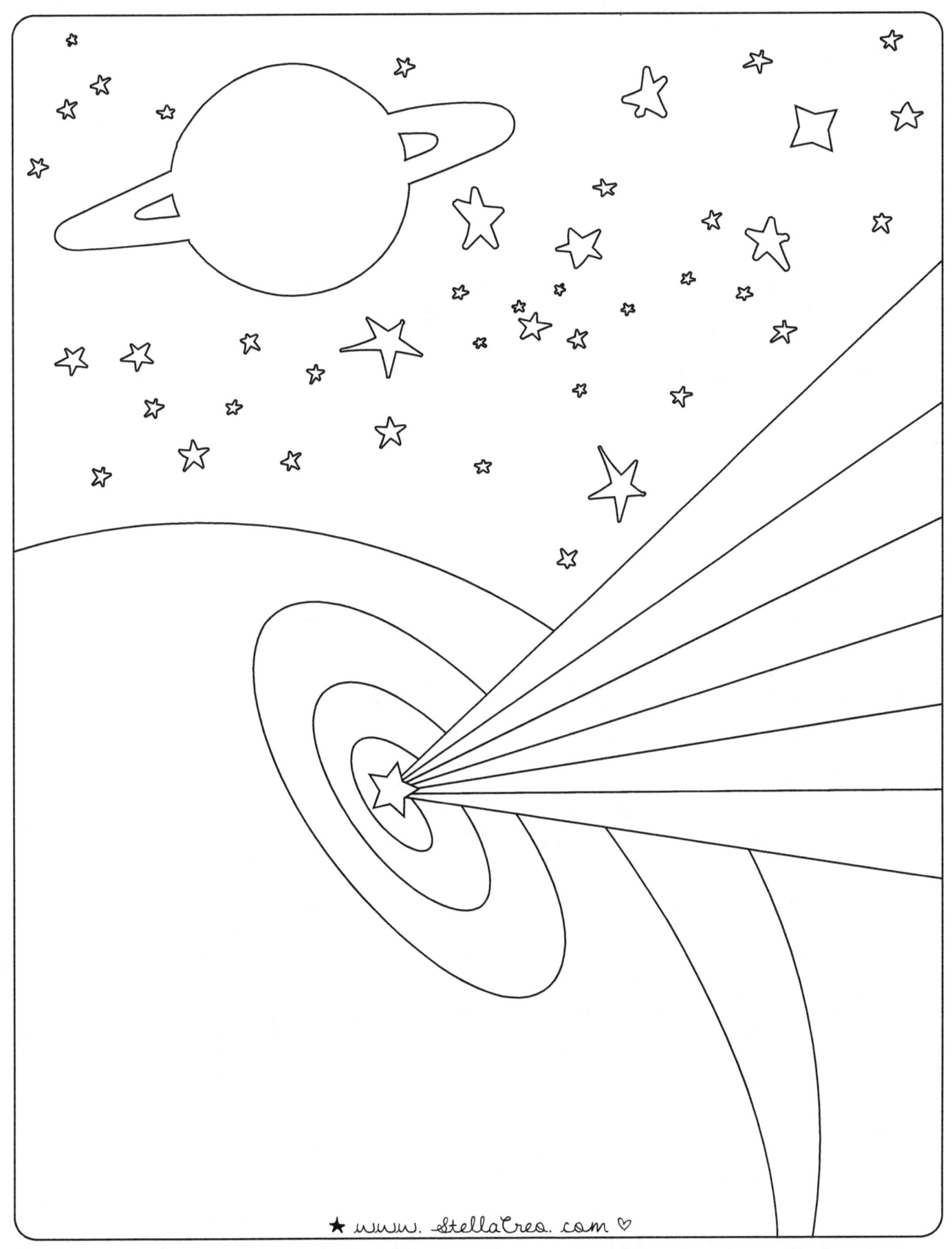

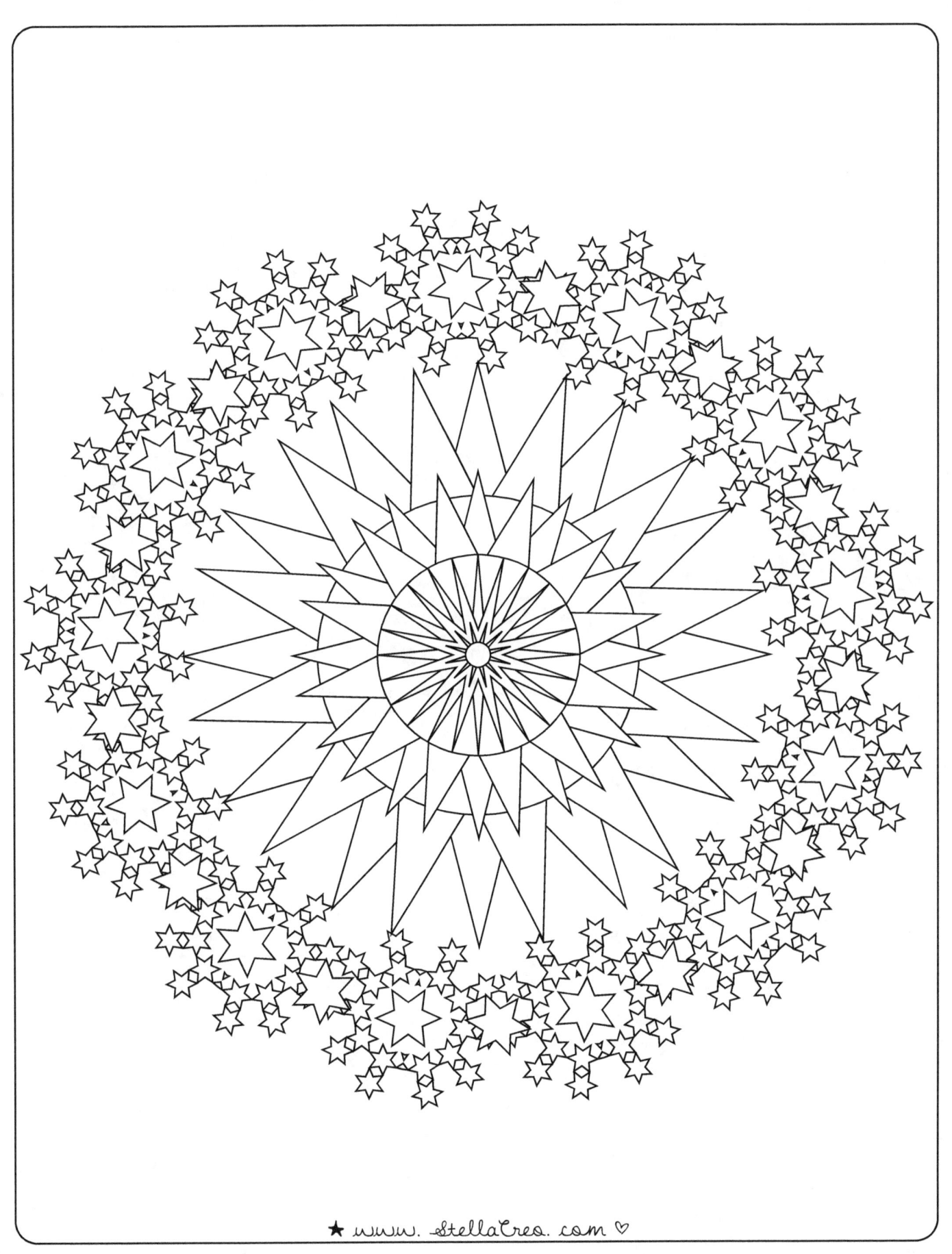

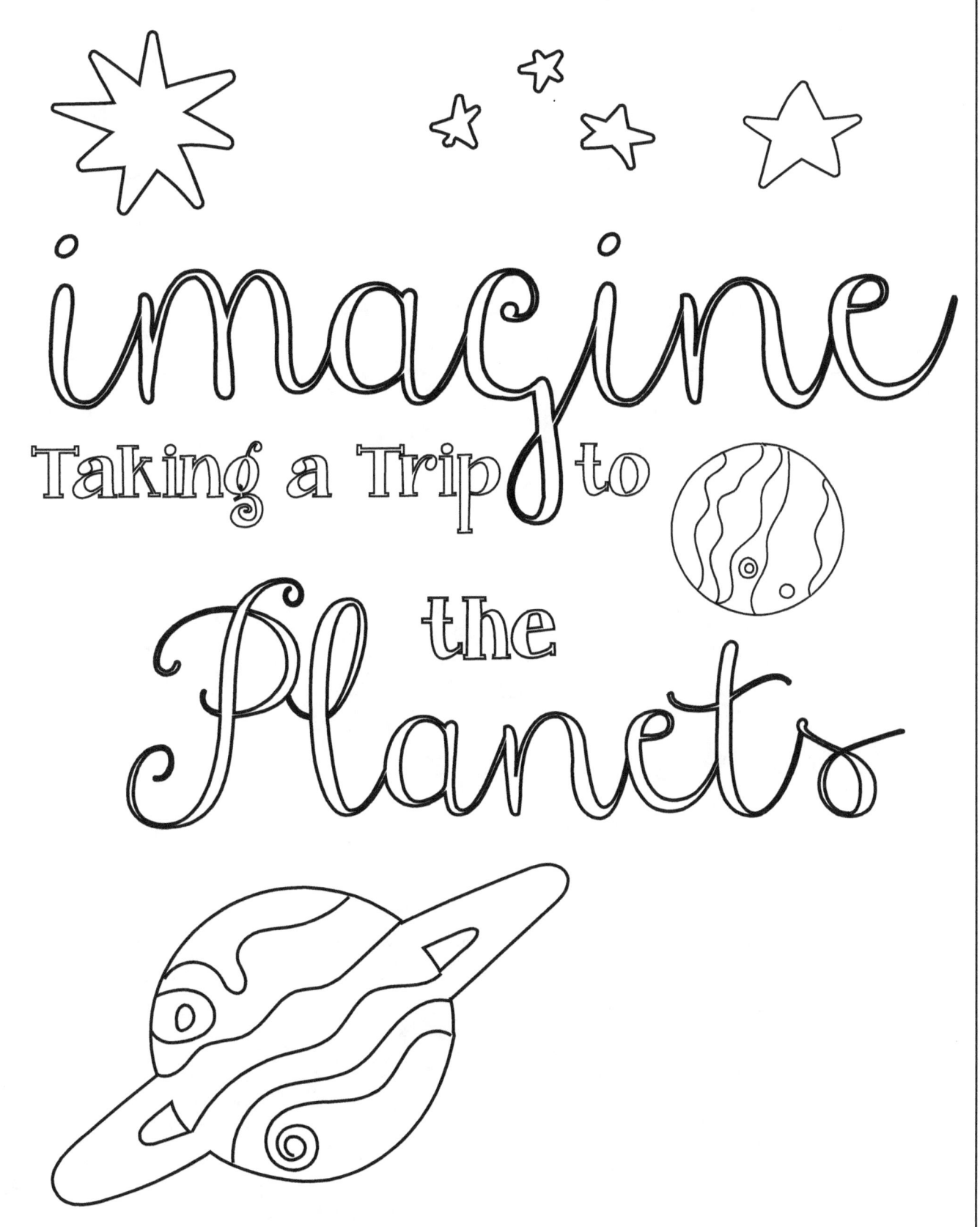

imagine
Taking a Trip to
the
Planets

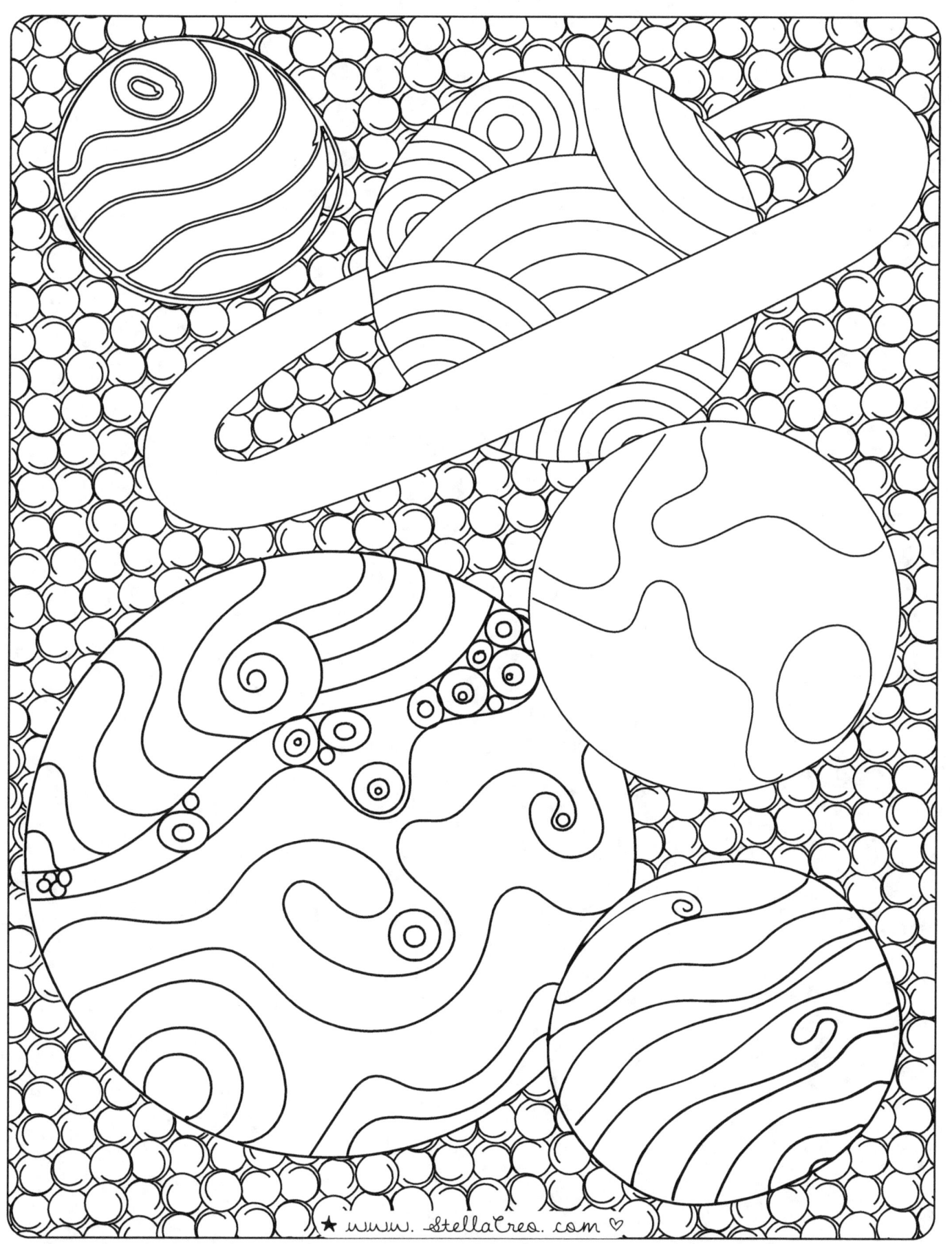

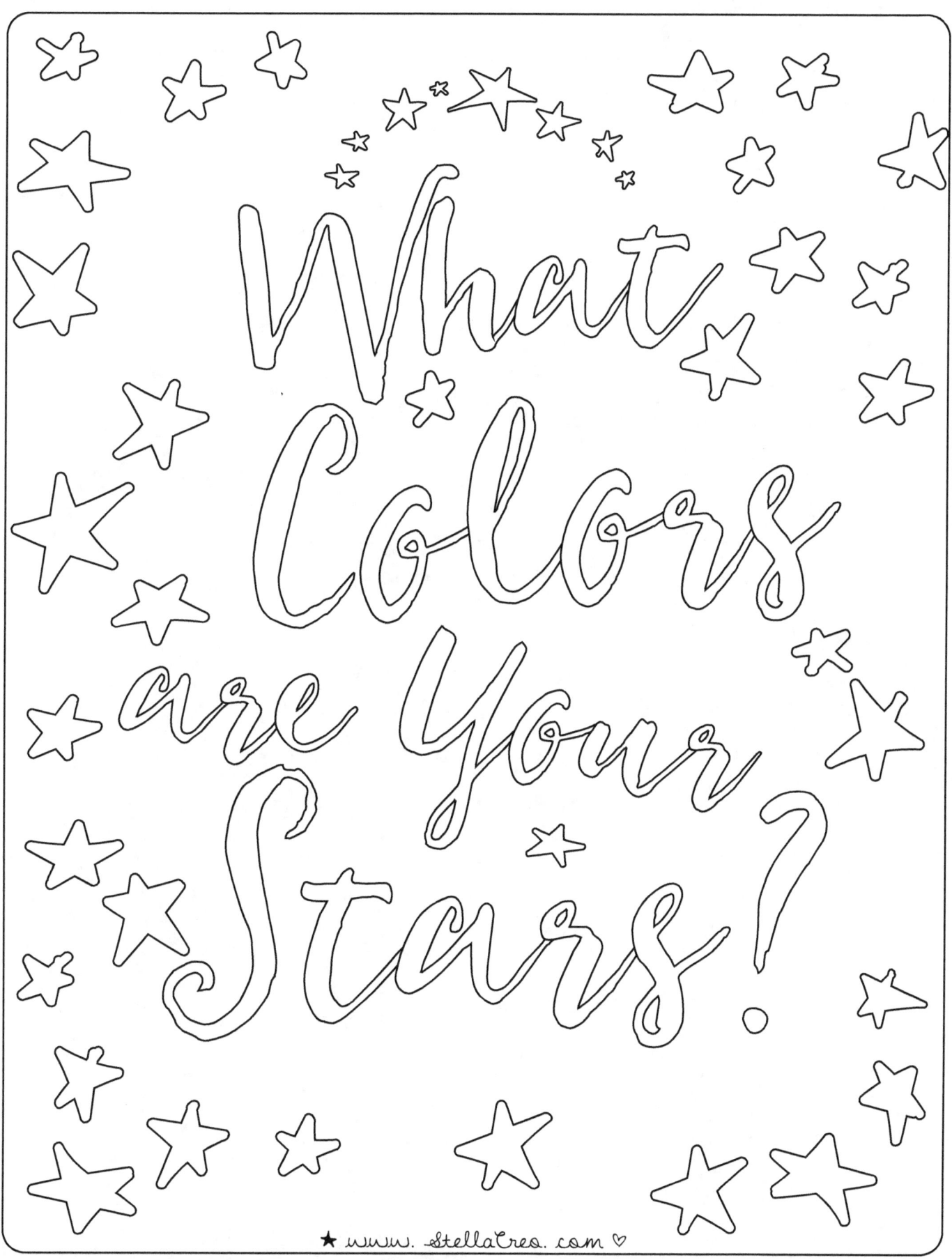

What Colors are Your Stars?

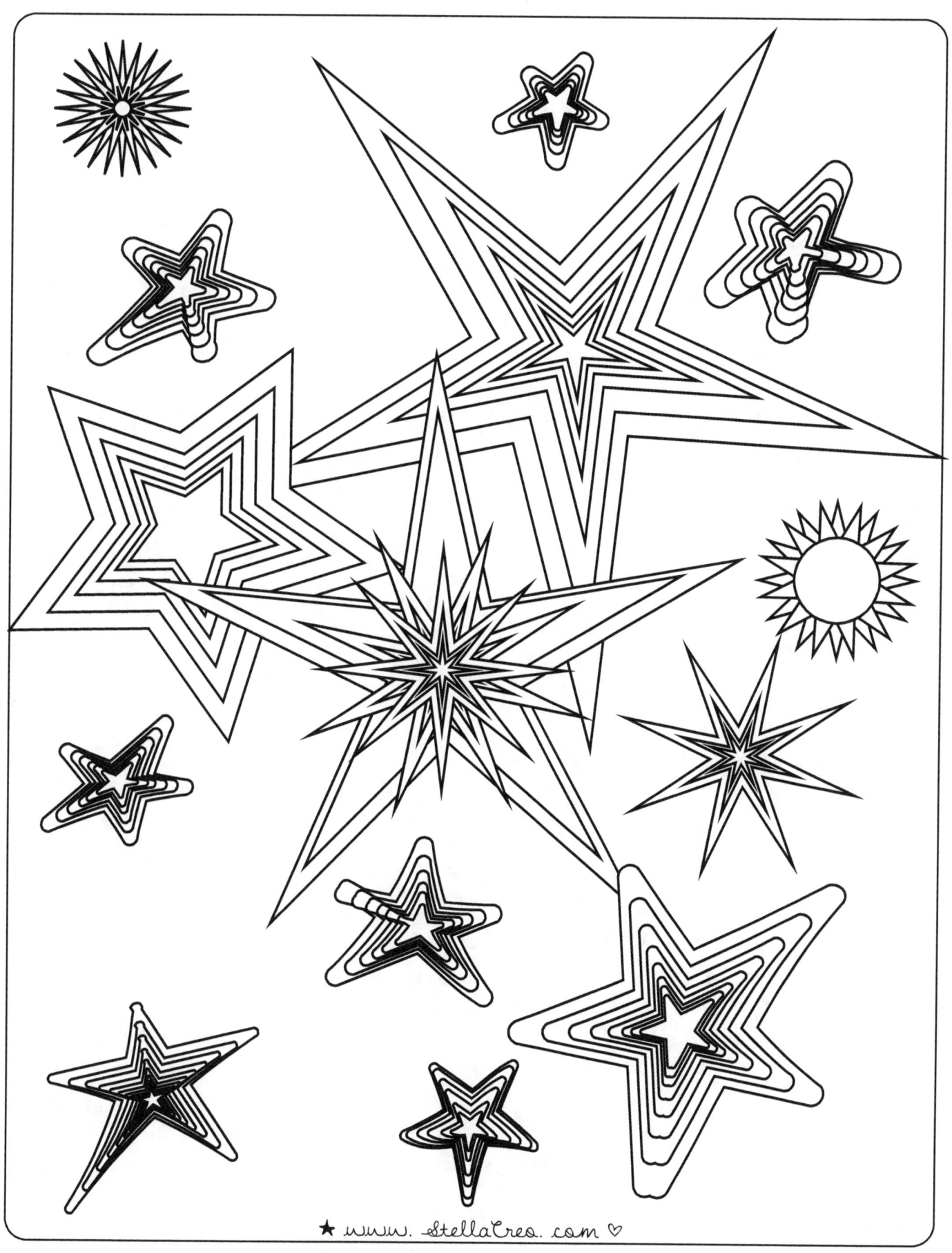

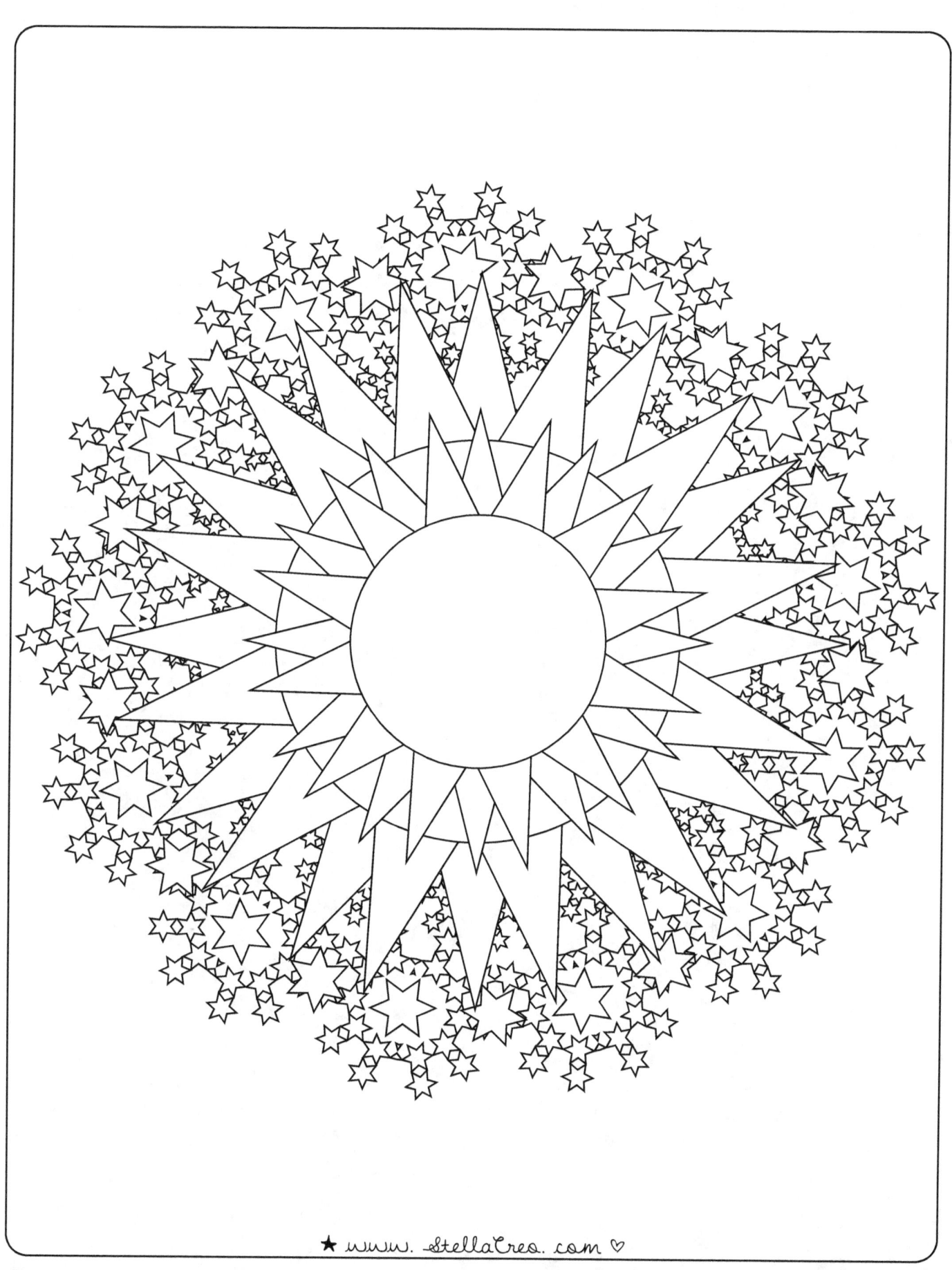

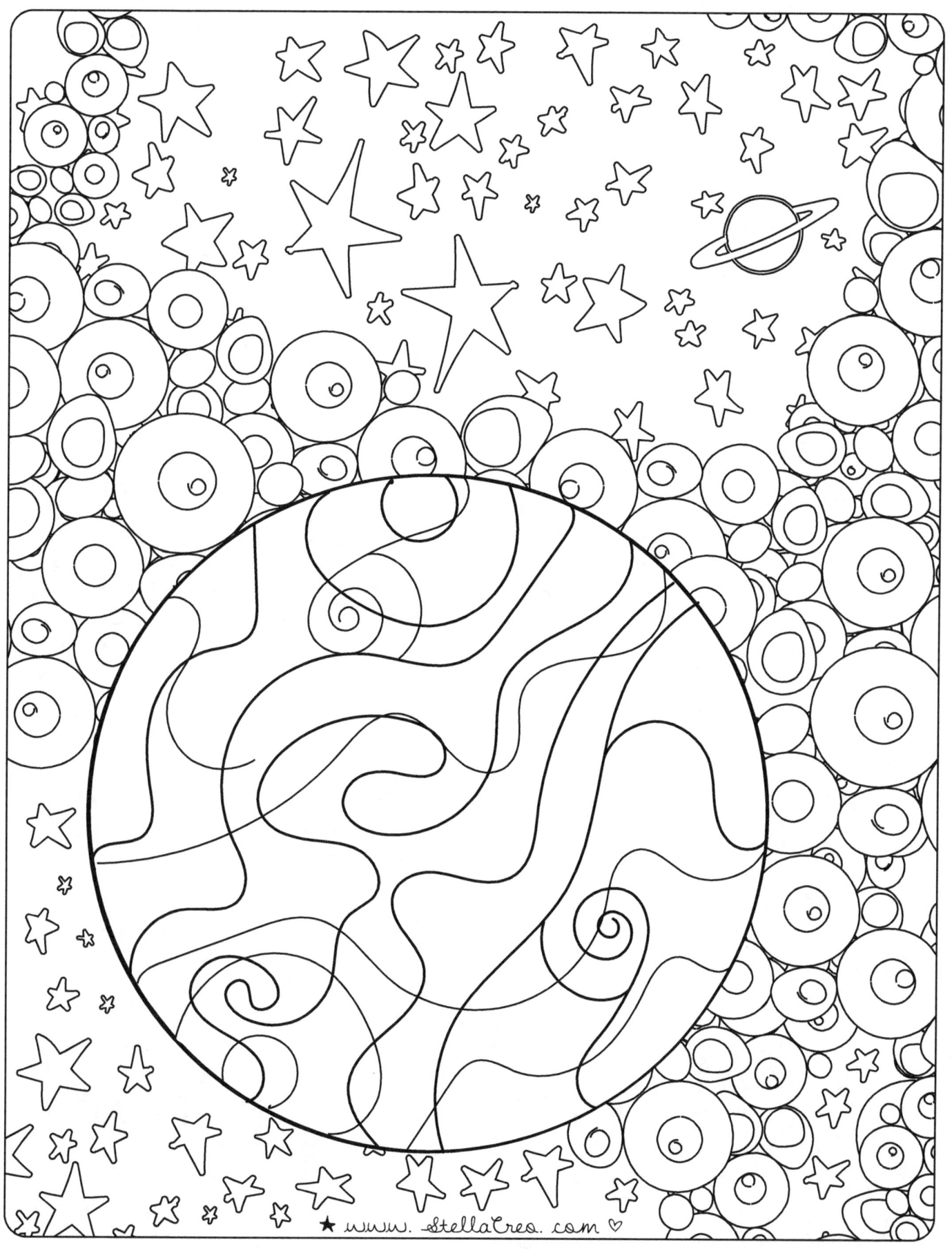

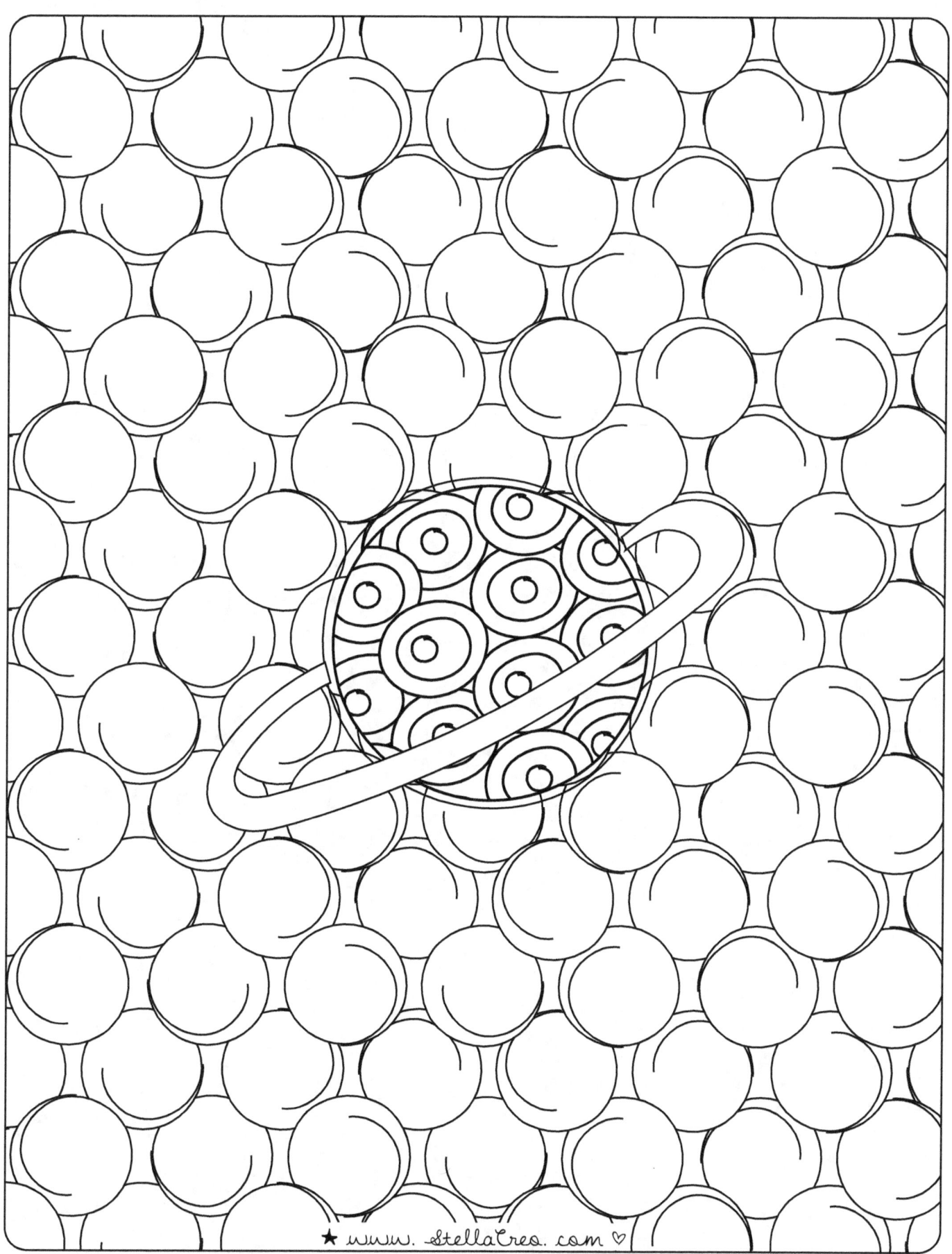

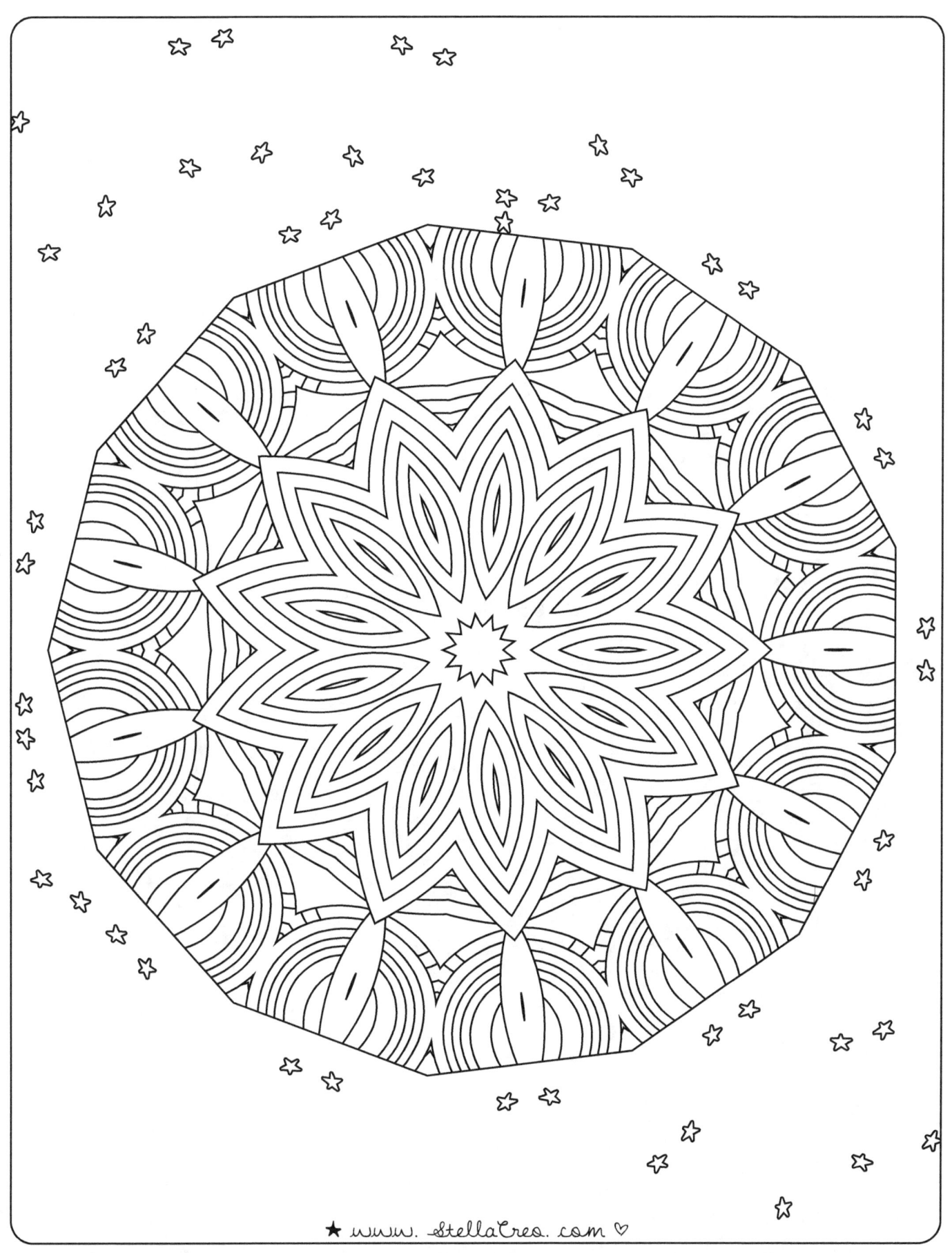

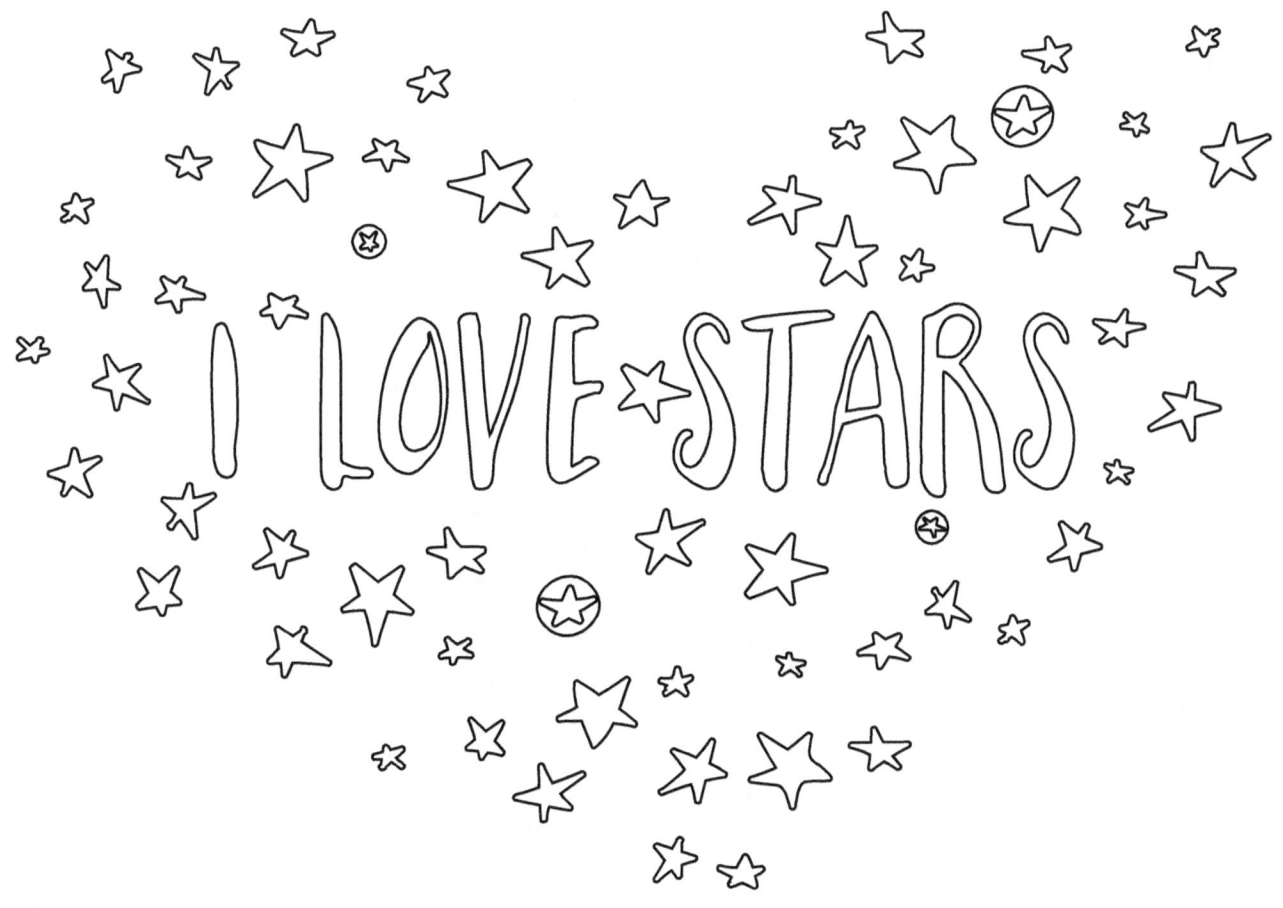

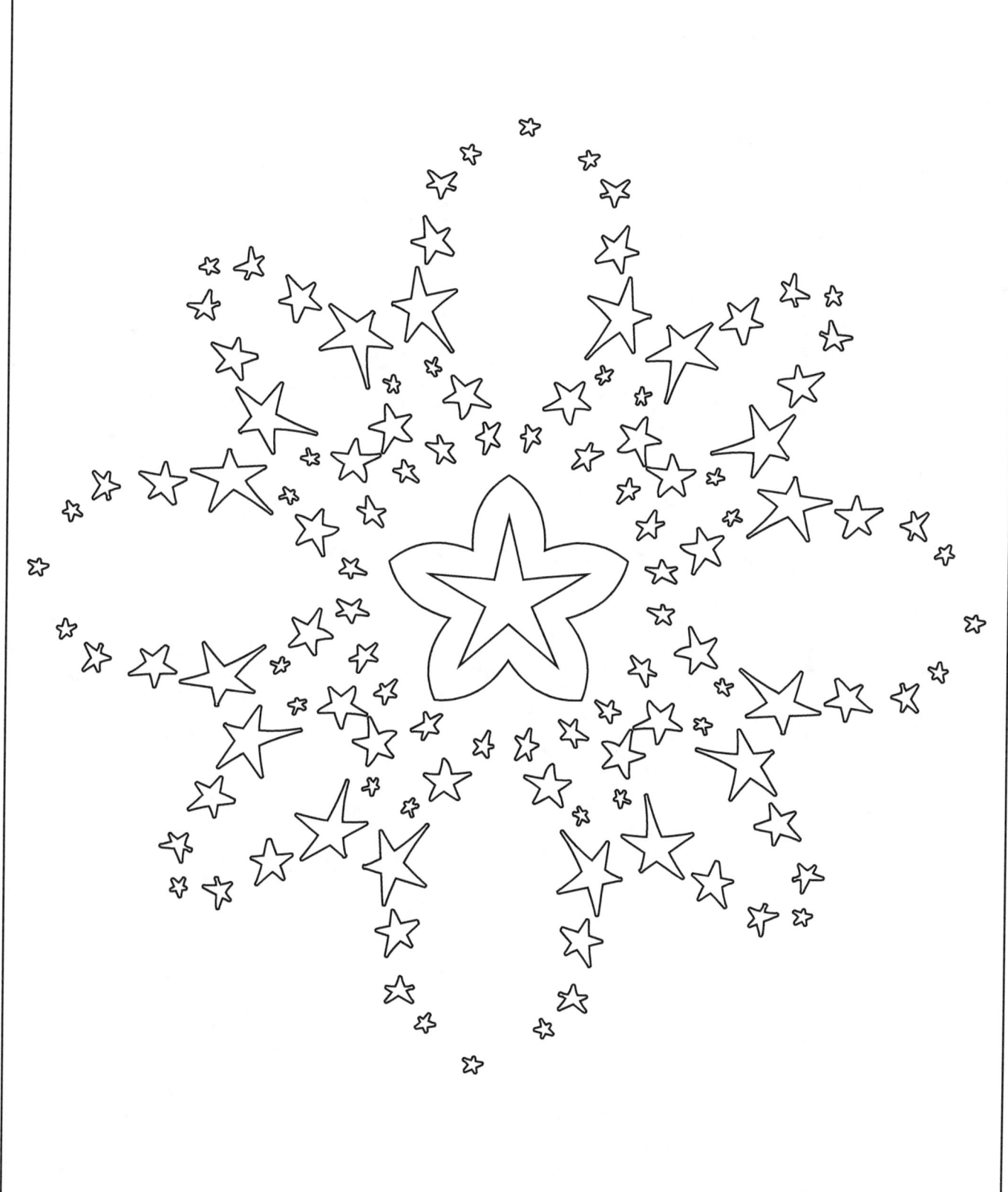

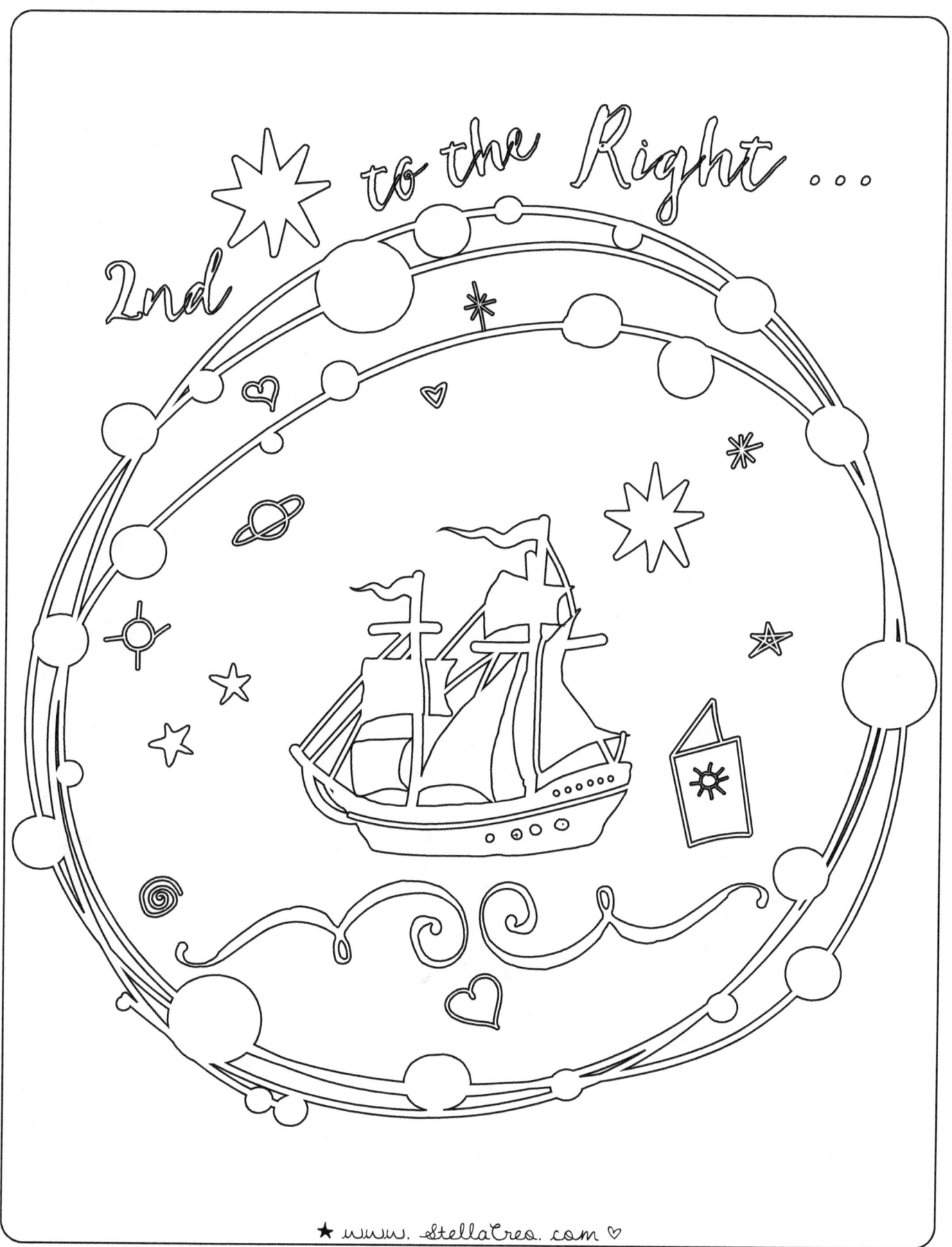

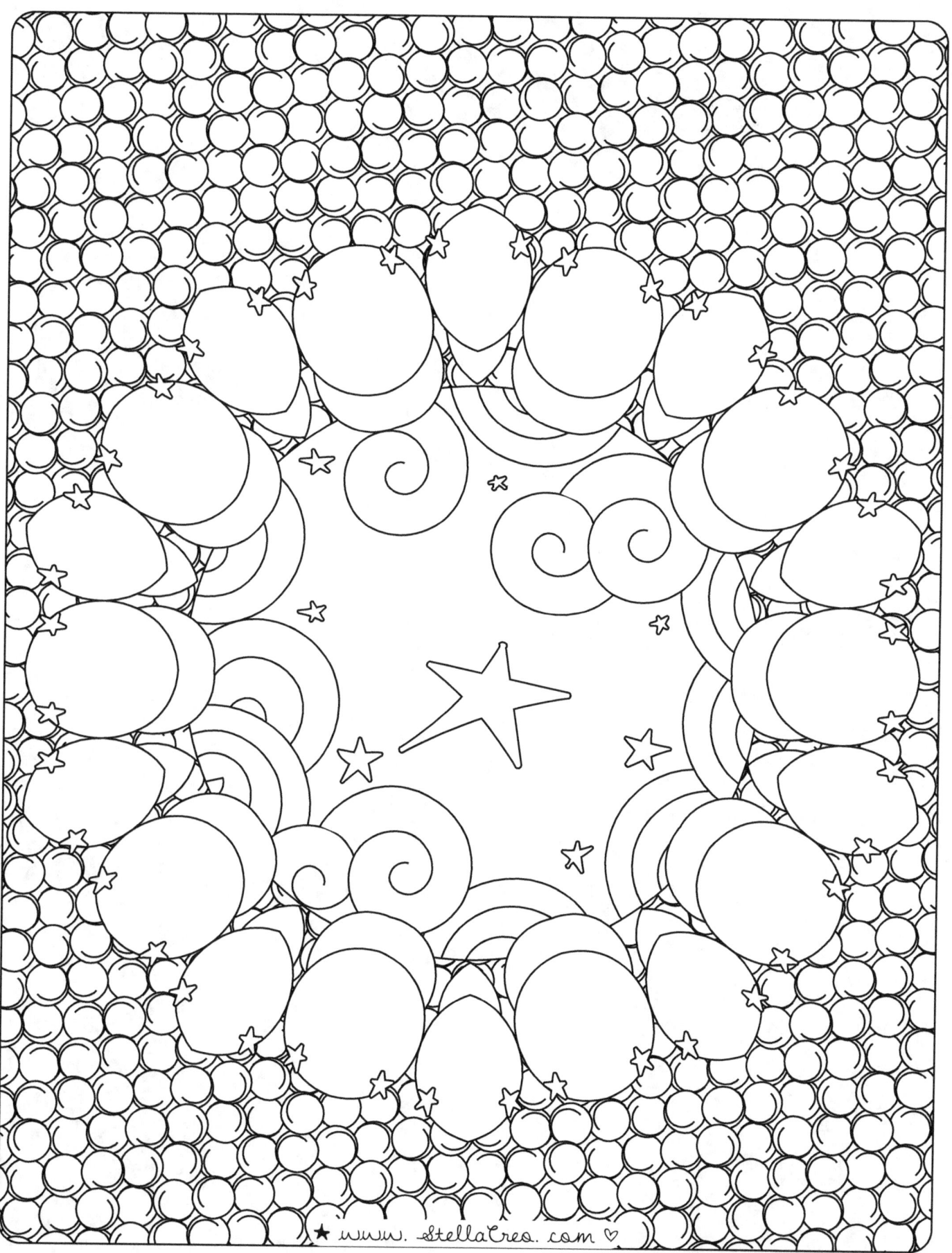

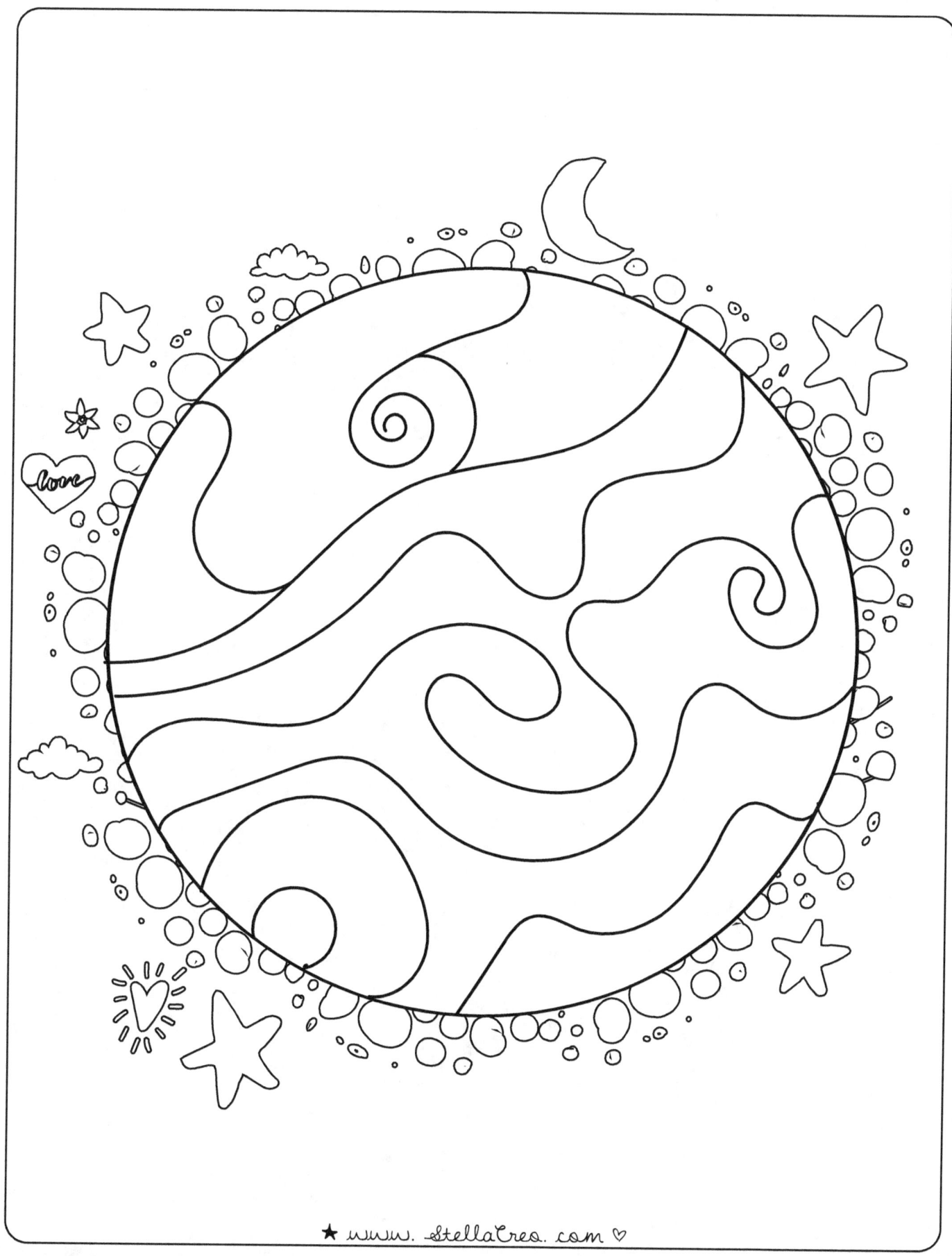

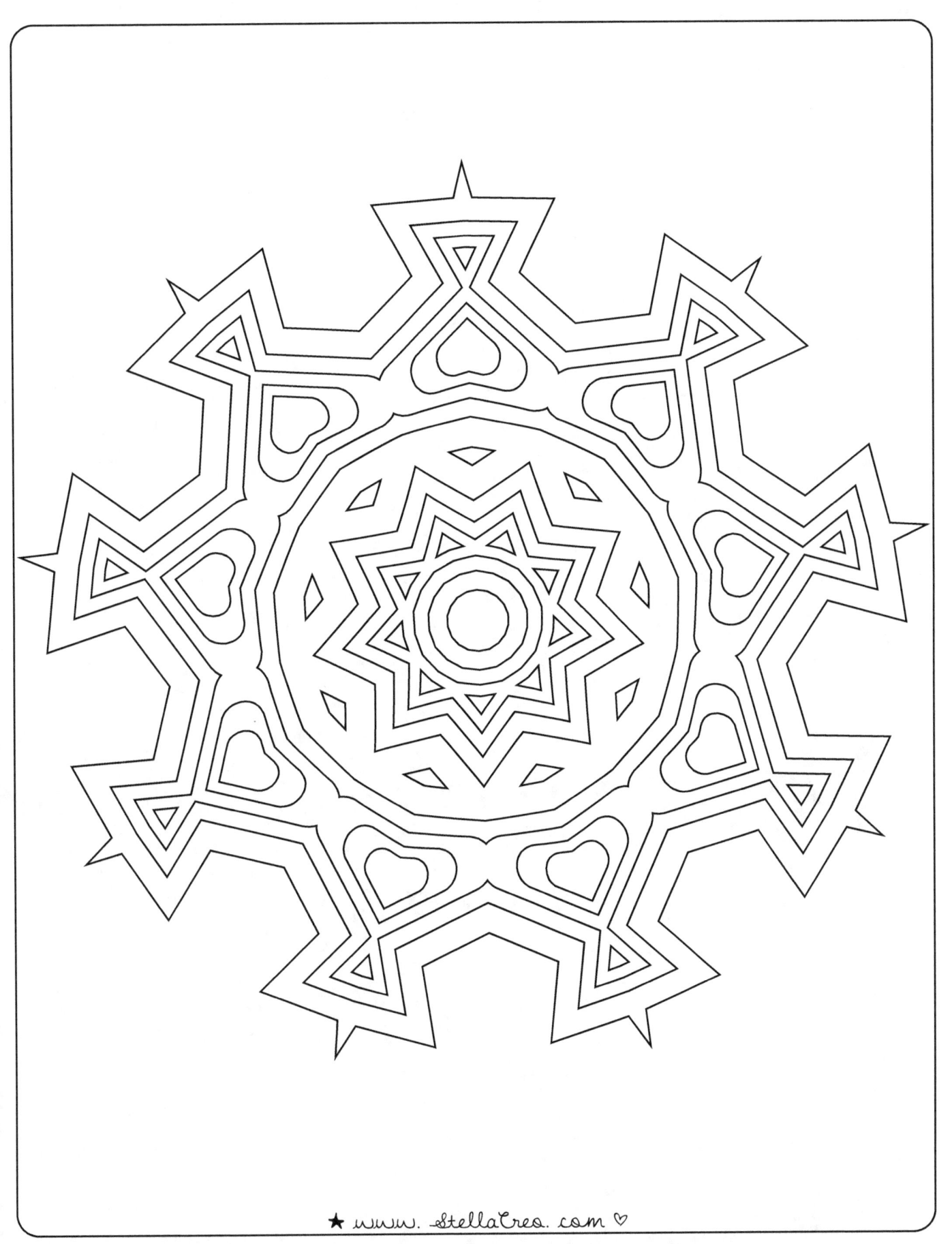

Rocket Engines

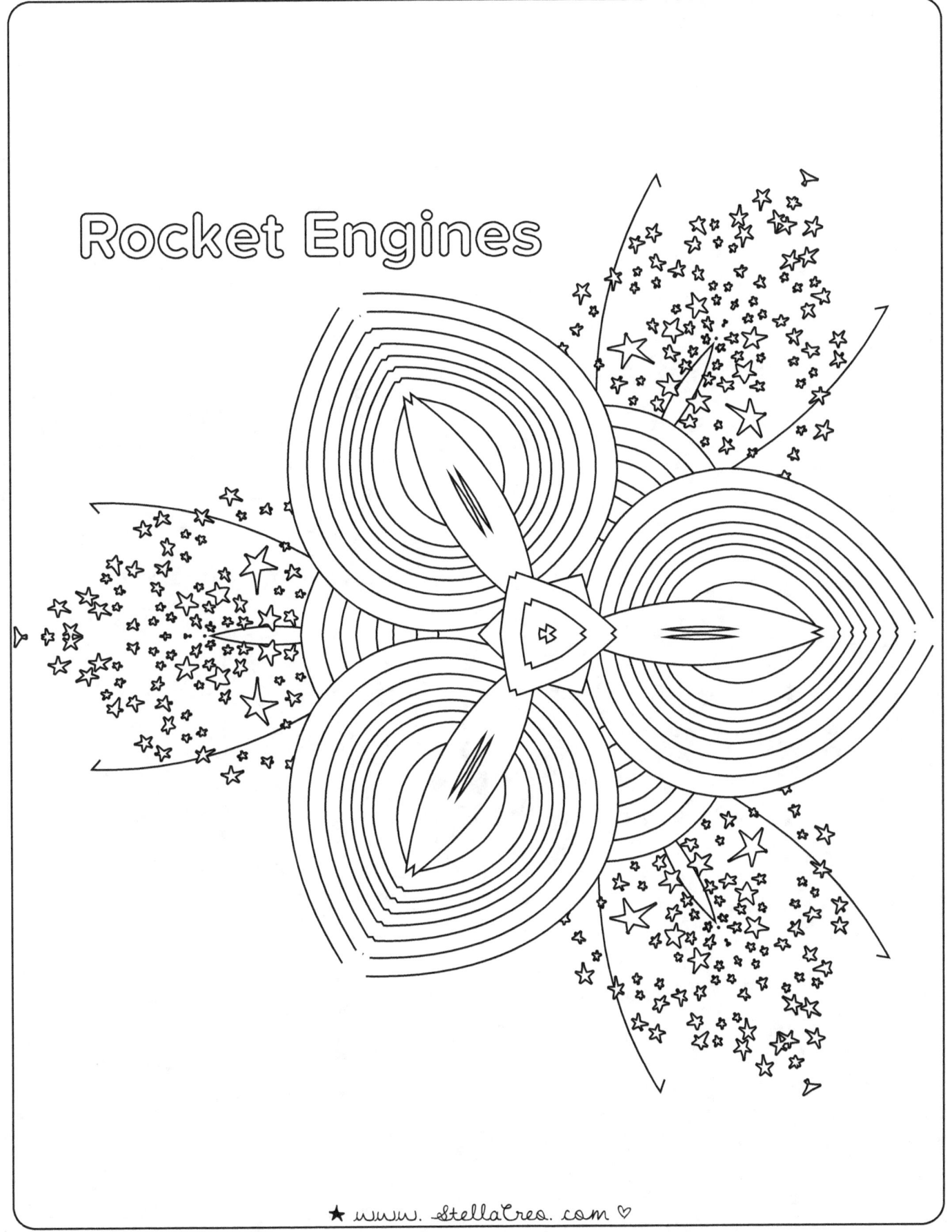

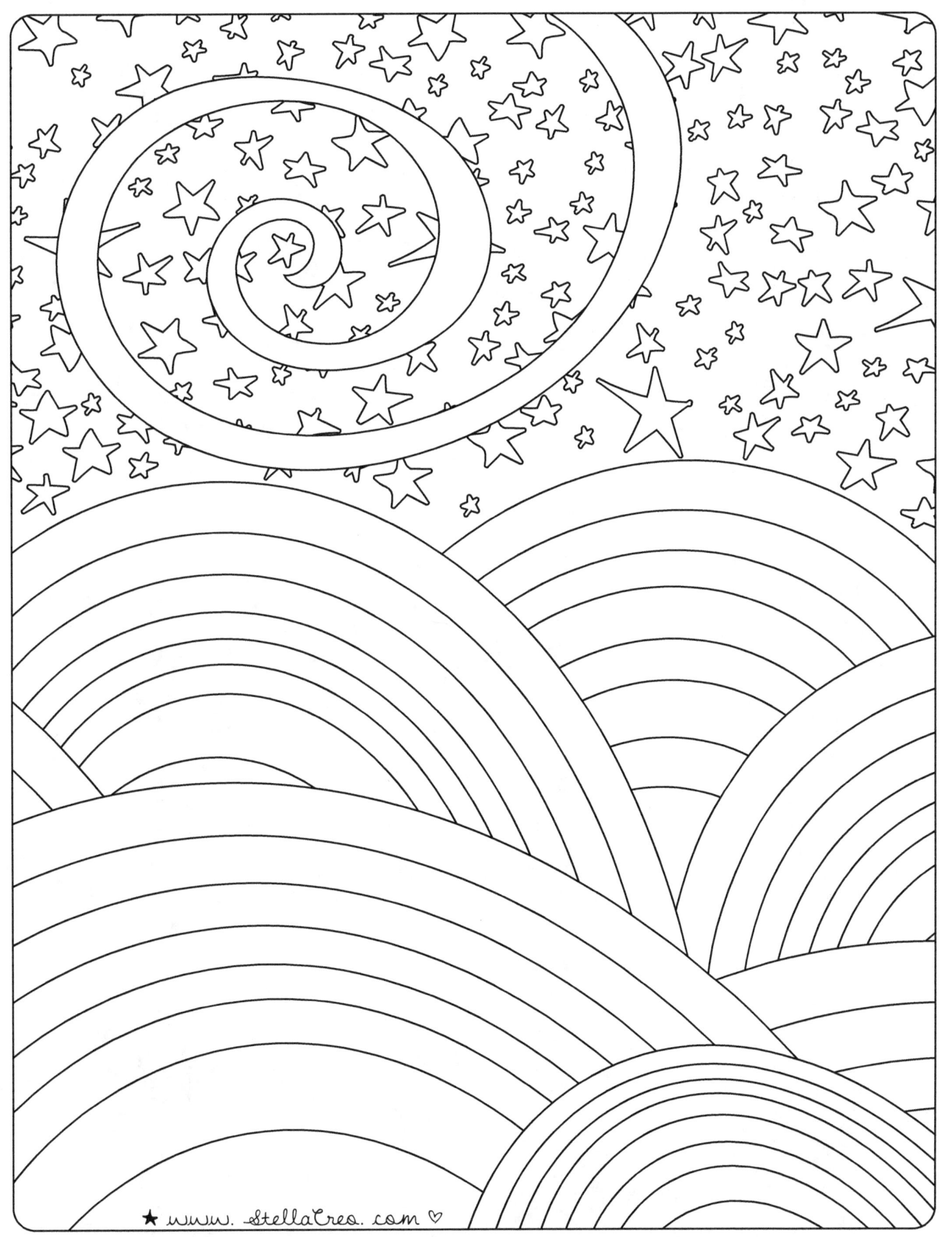

★ www. StellaCrea. com ♡

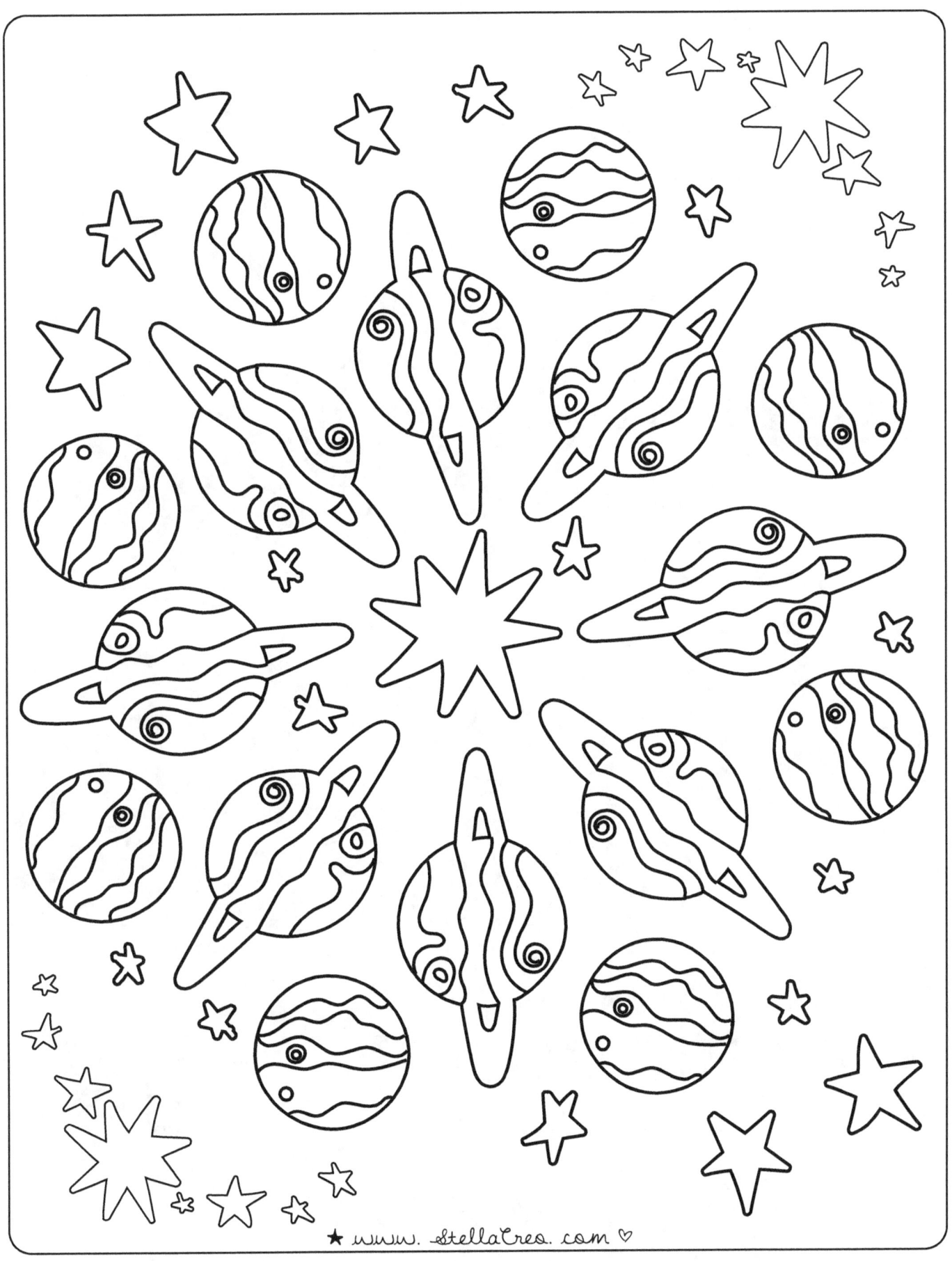

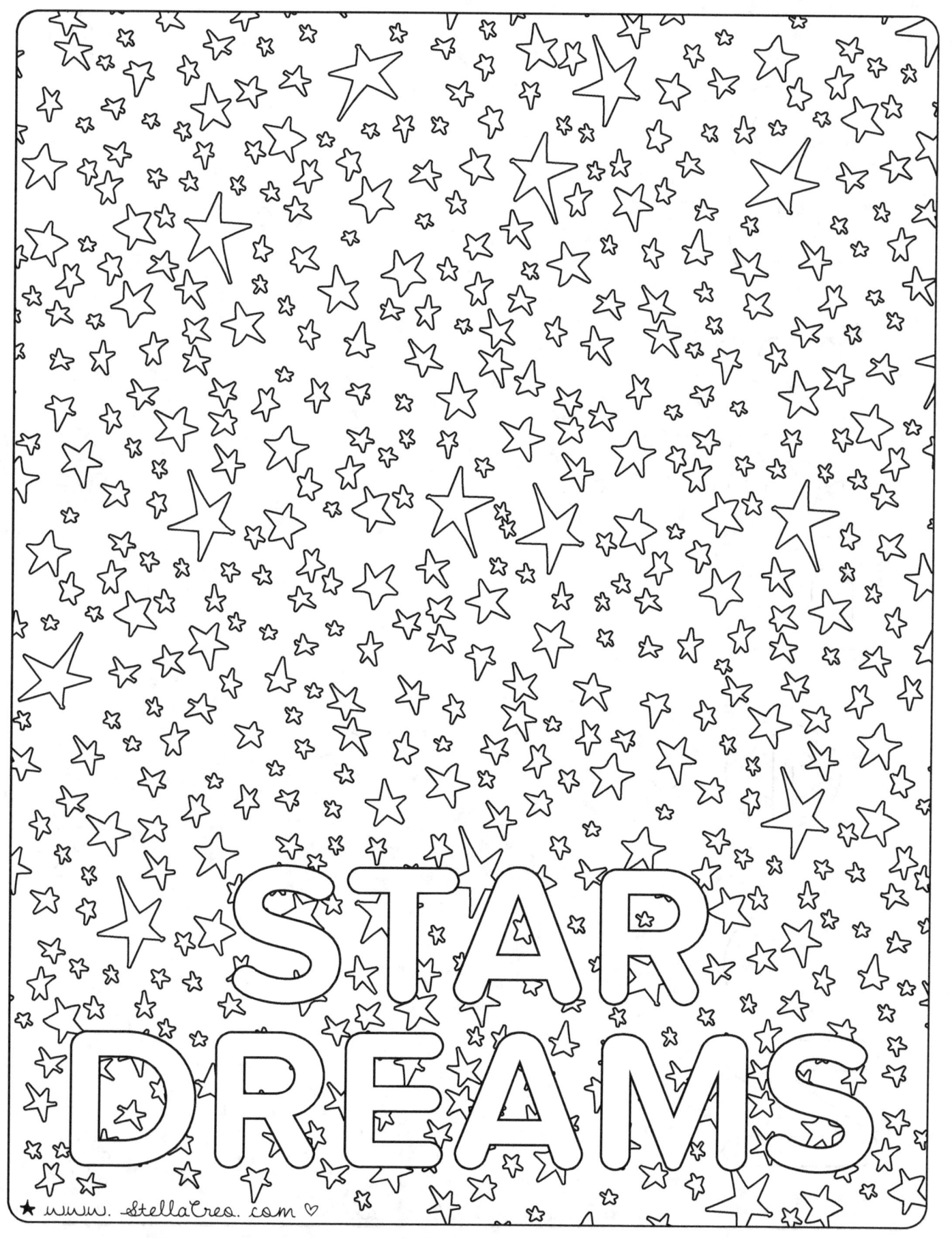

STAR
DREAMS

www.stellacrea.com

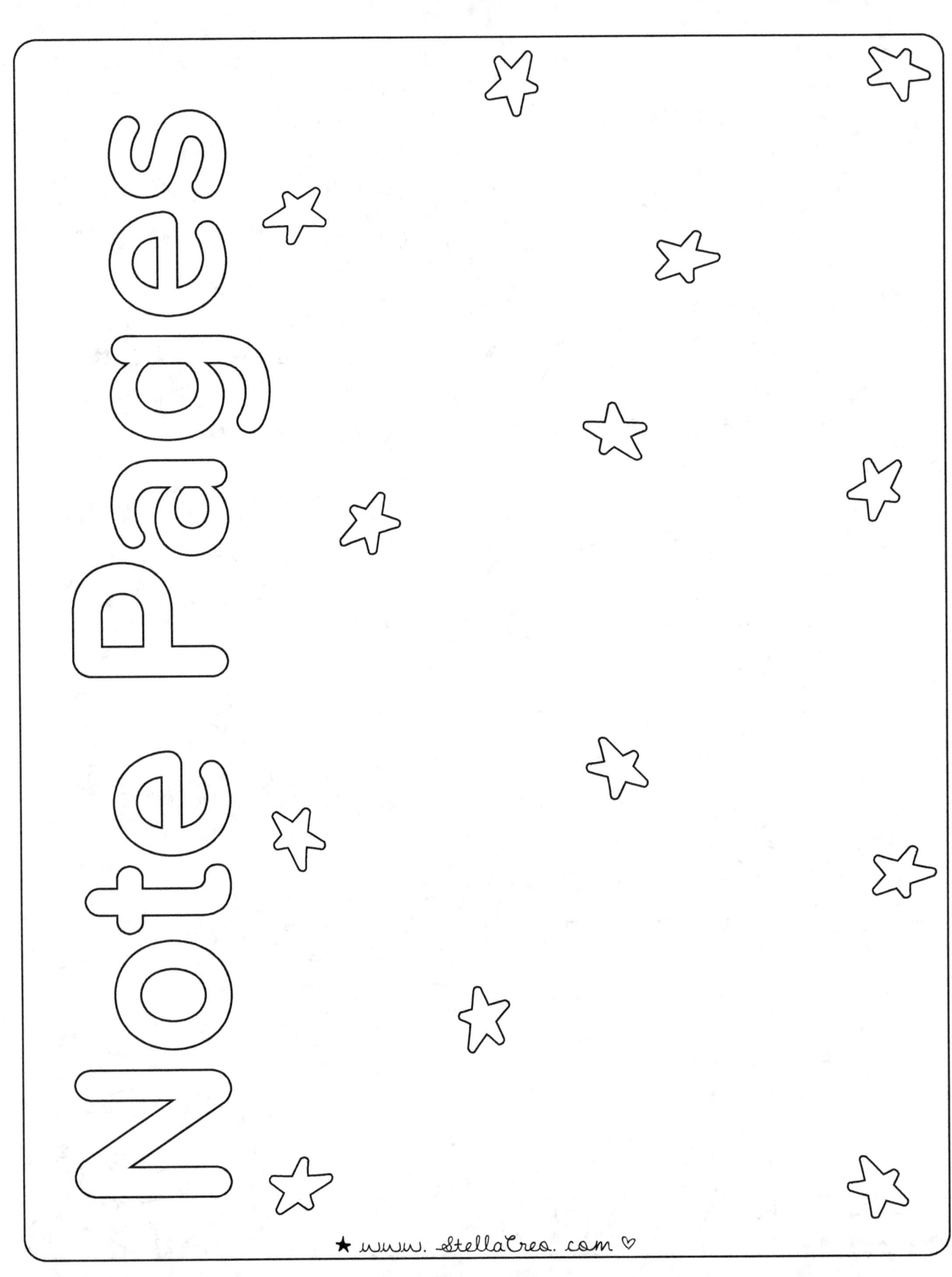

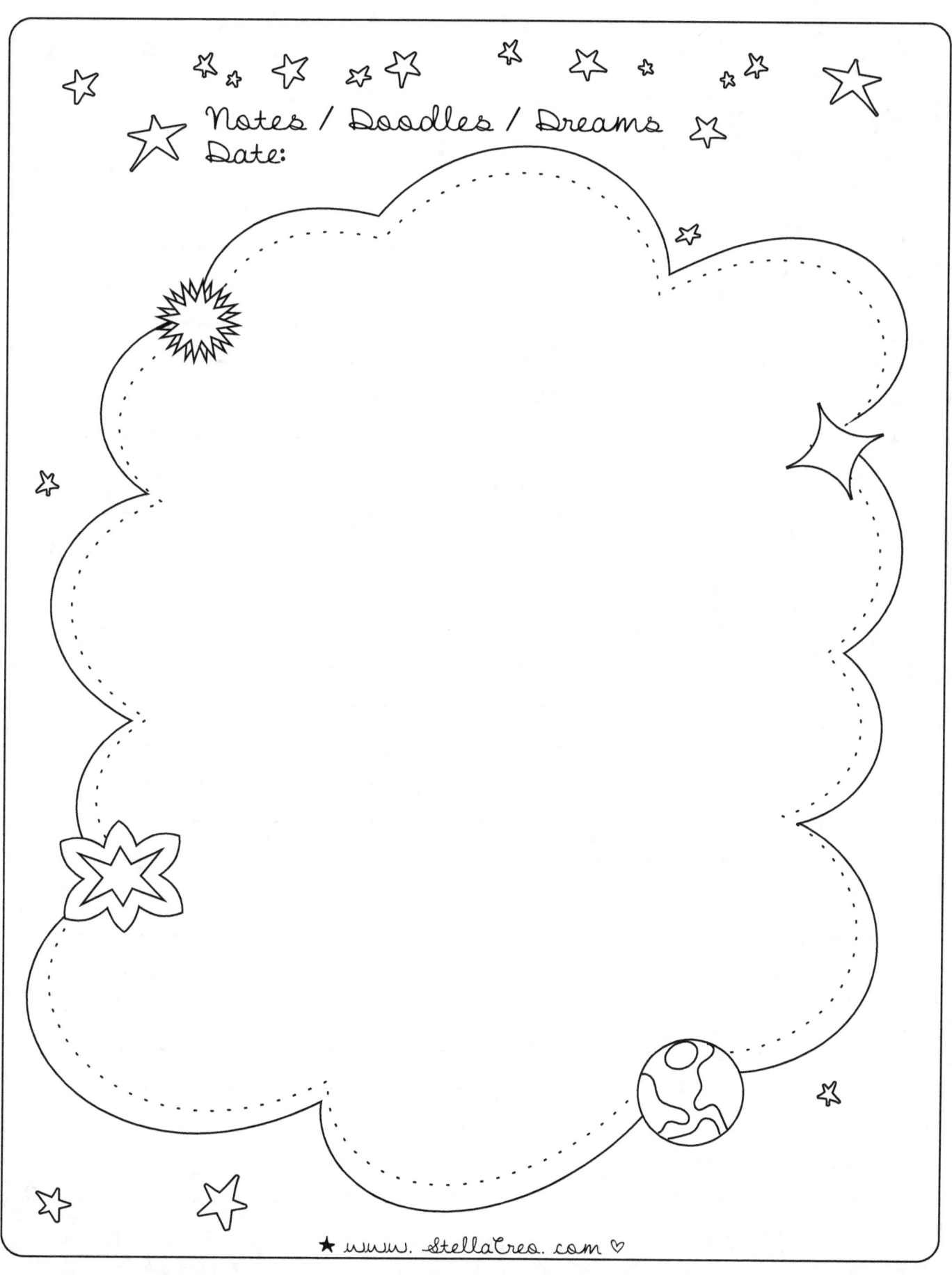

Notes / Doodles / Dreams
Date:

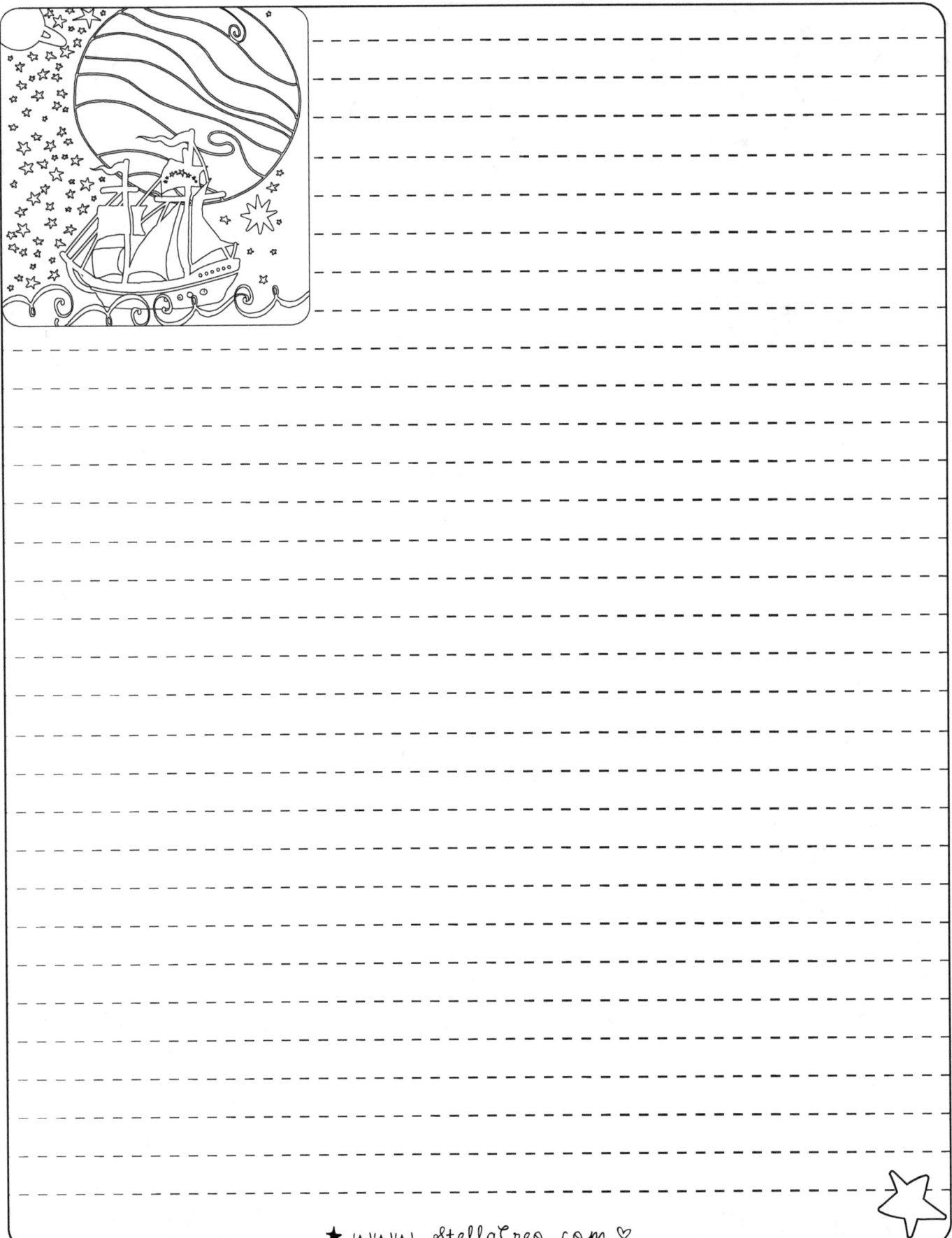

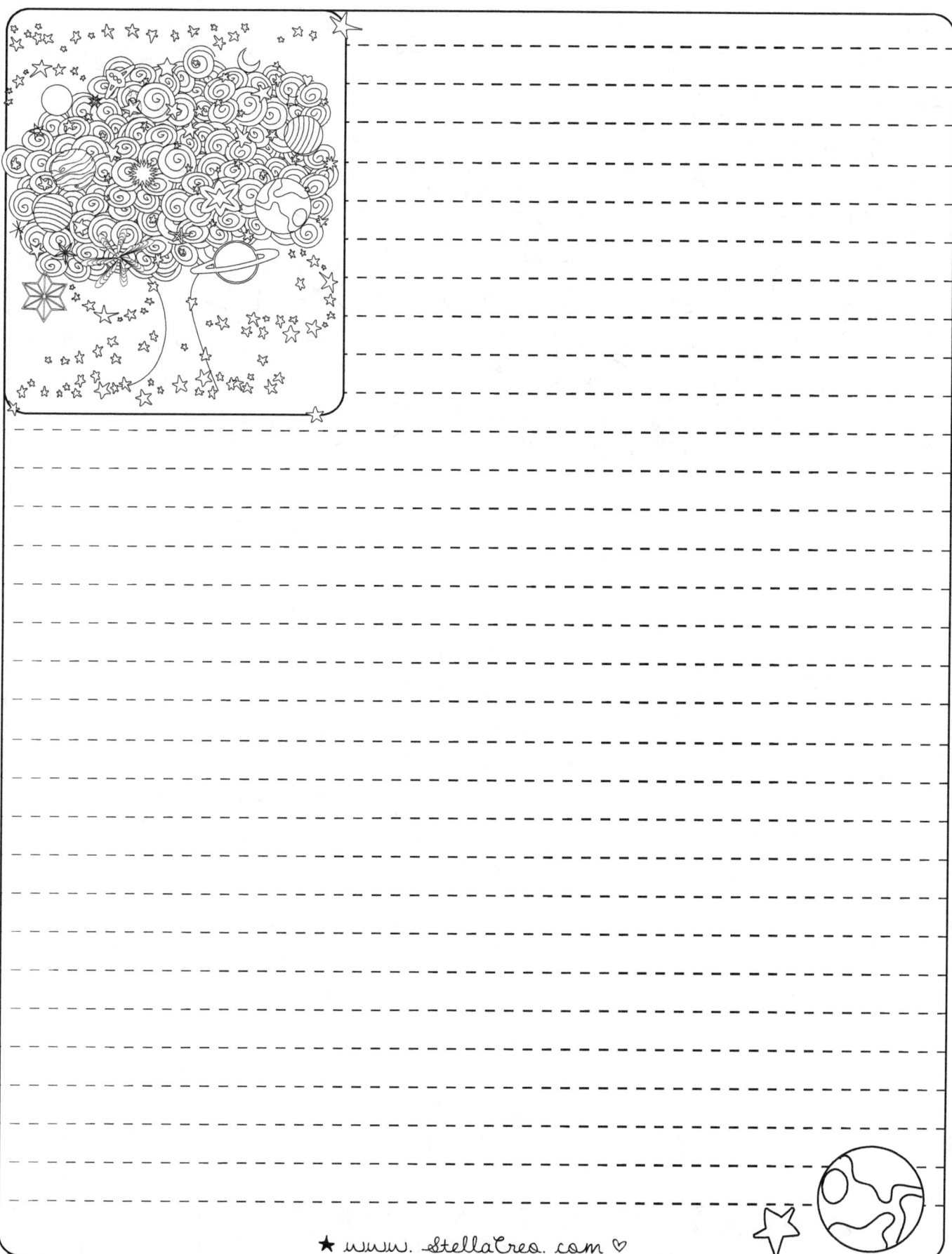

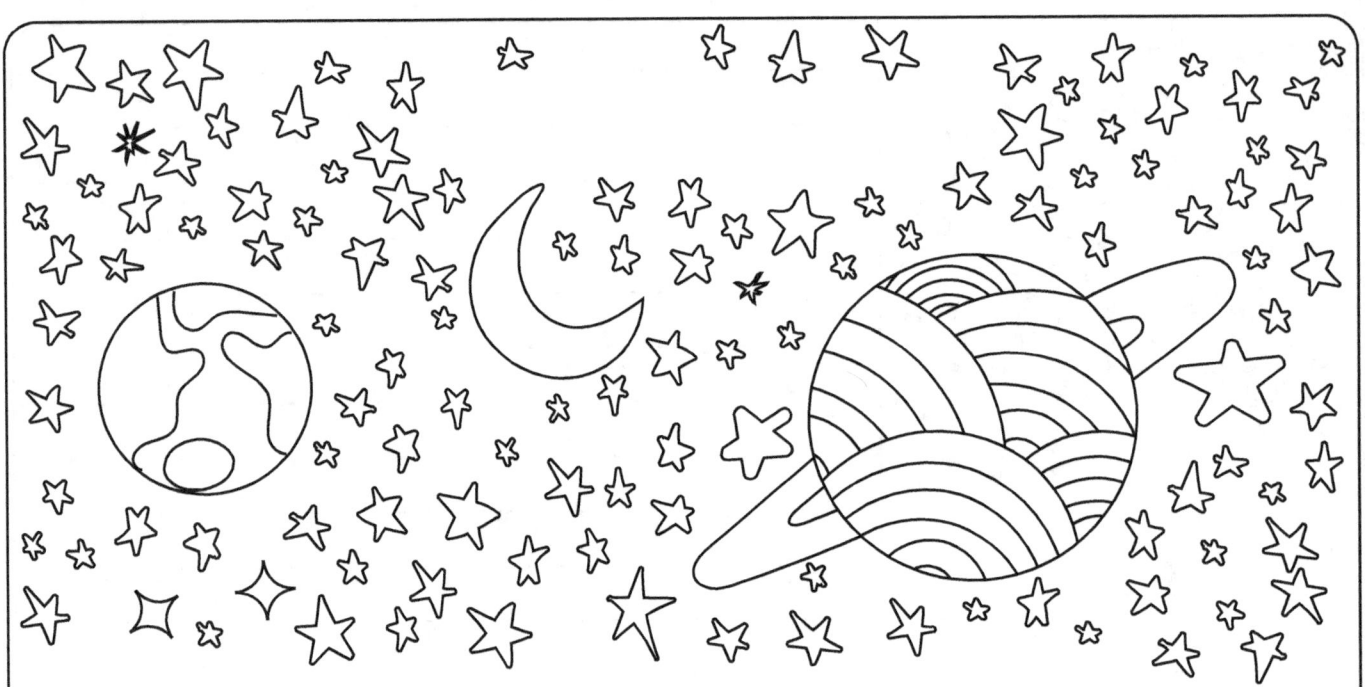

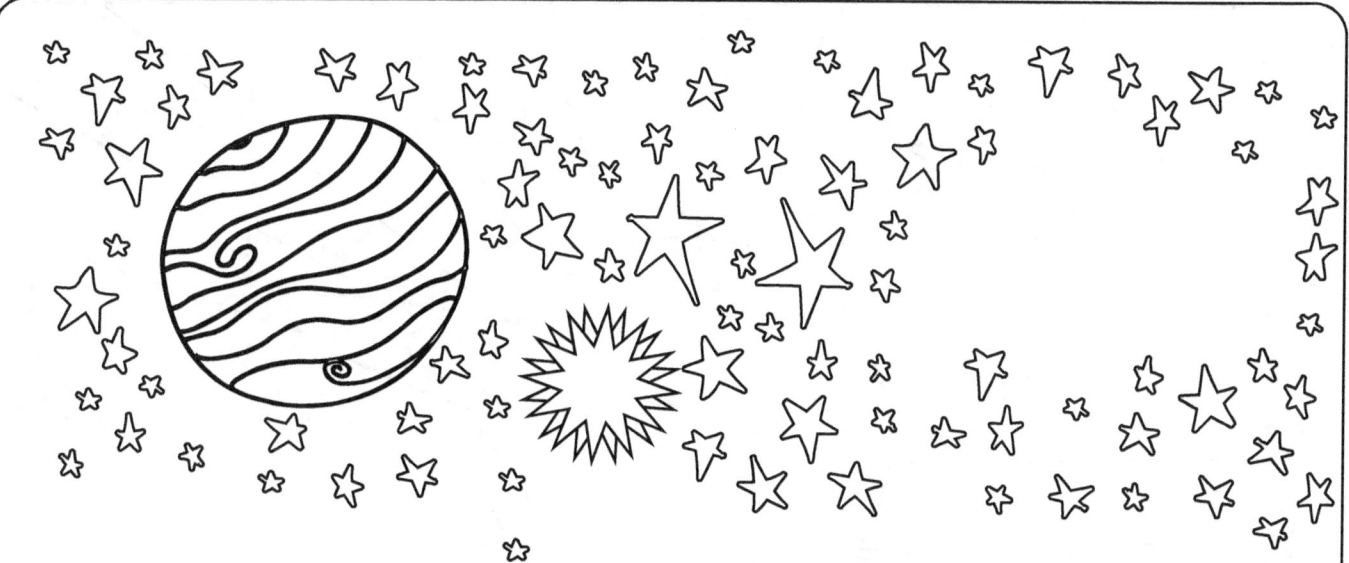

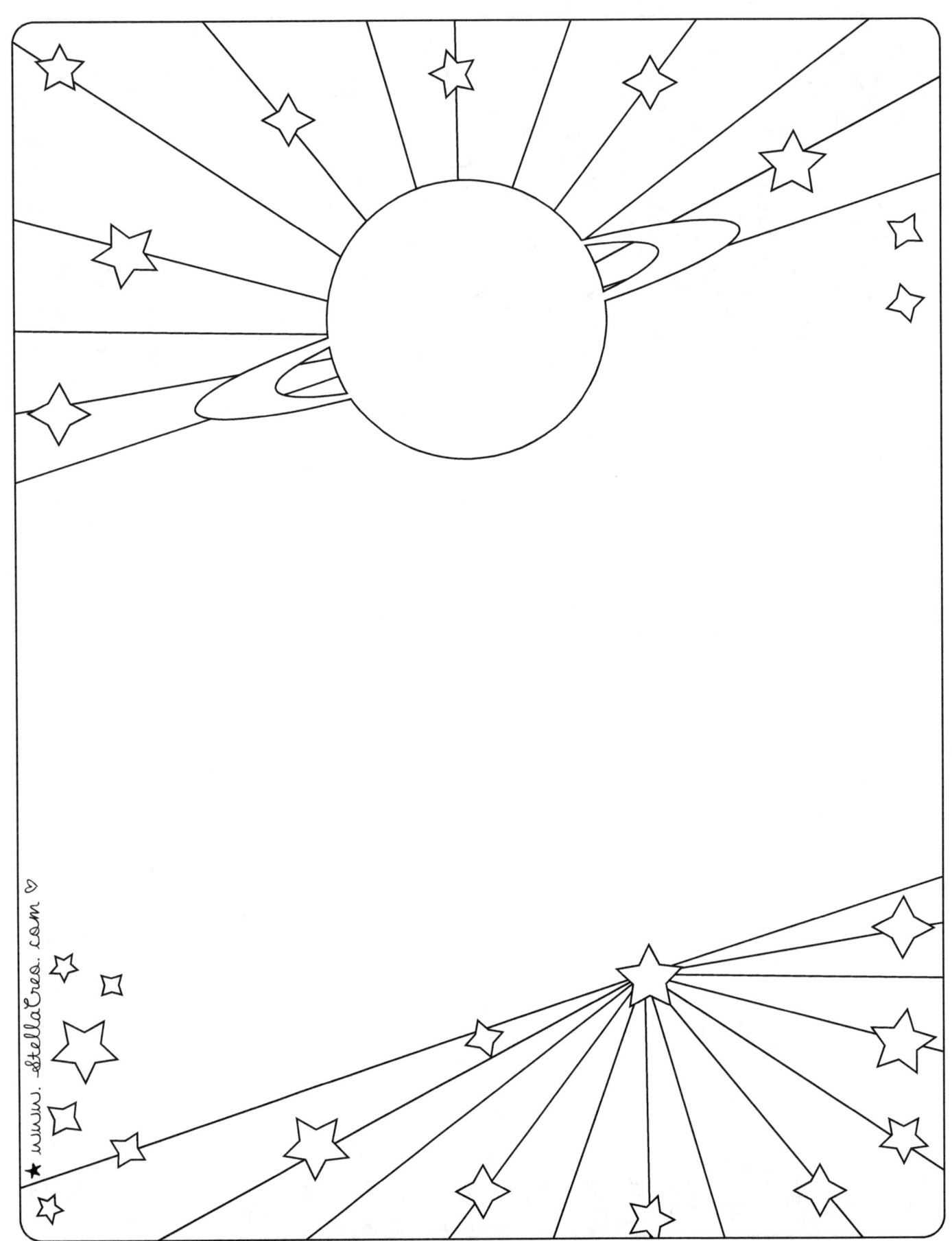

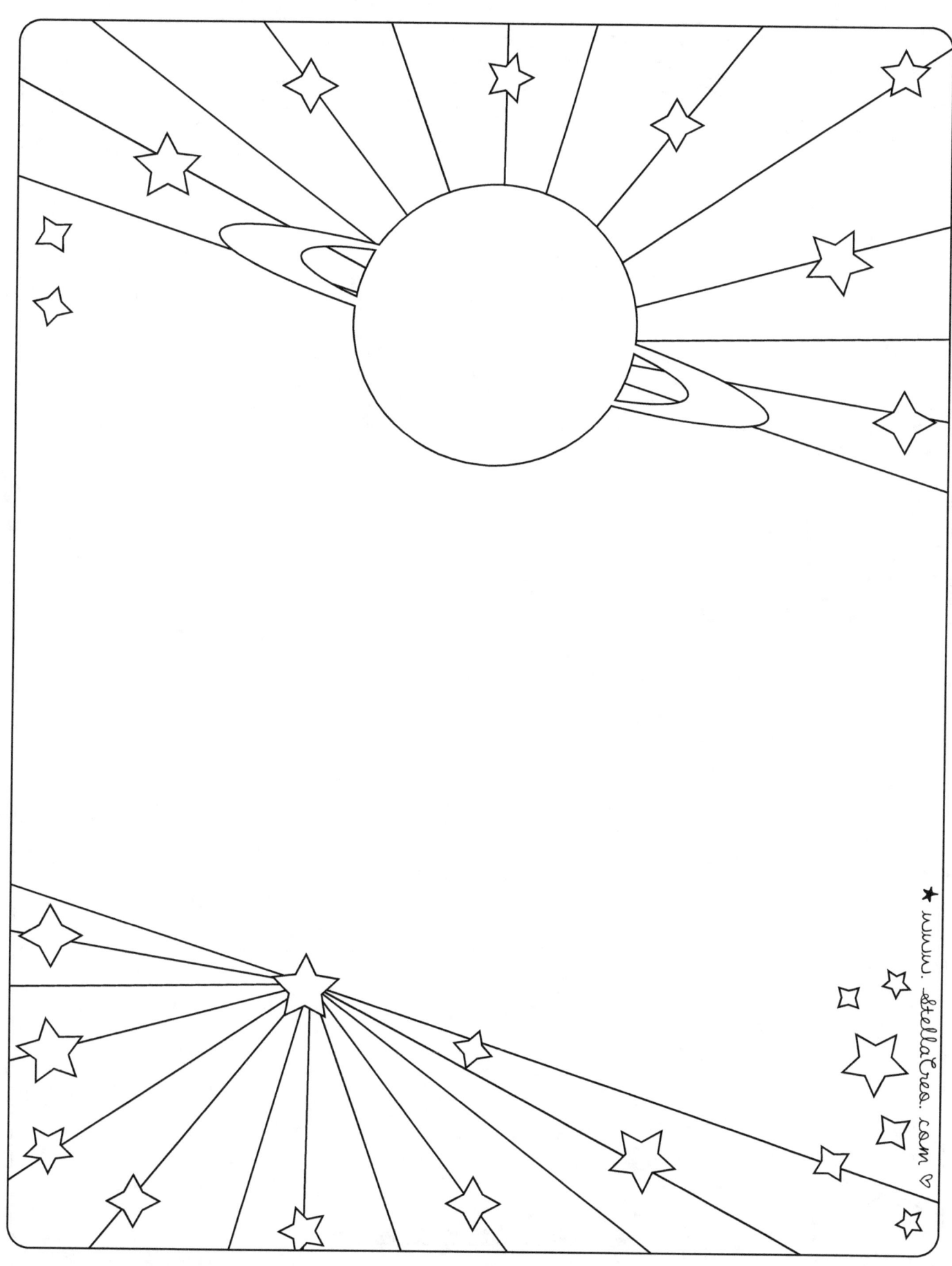

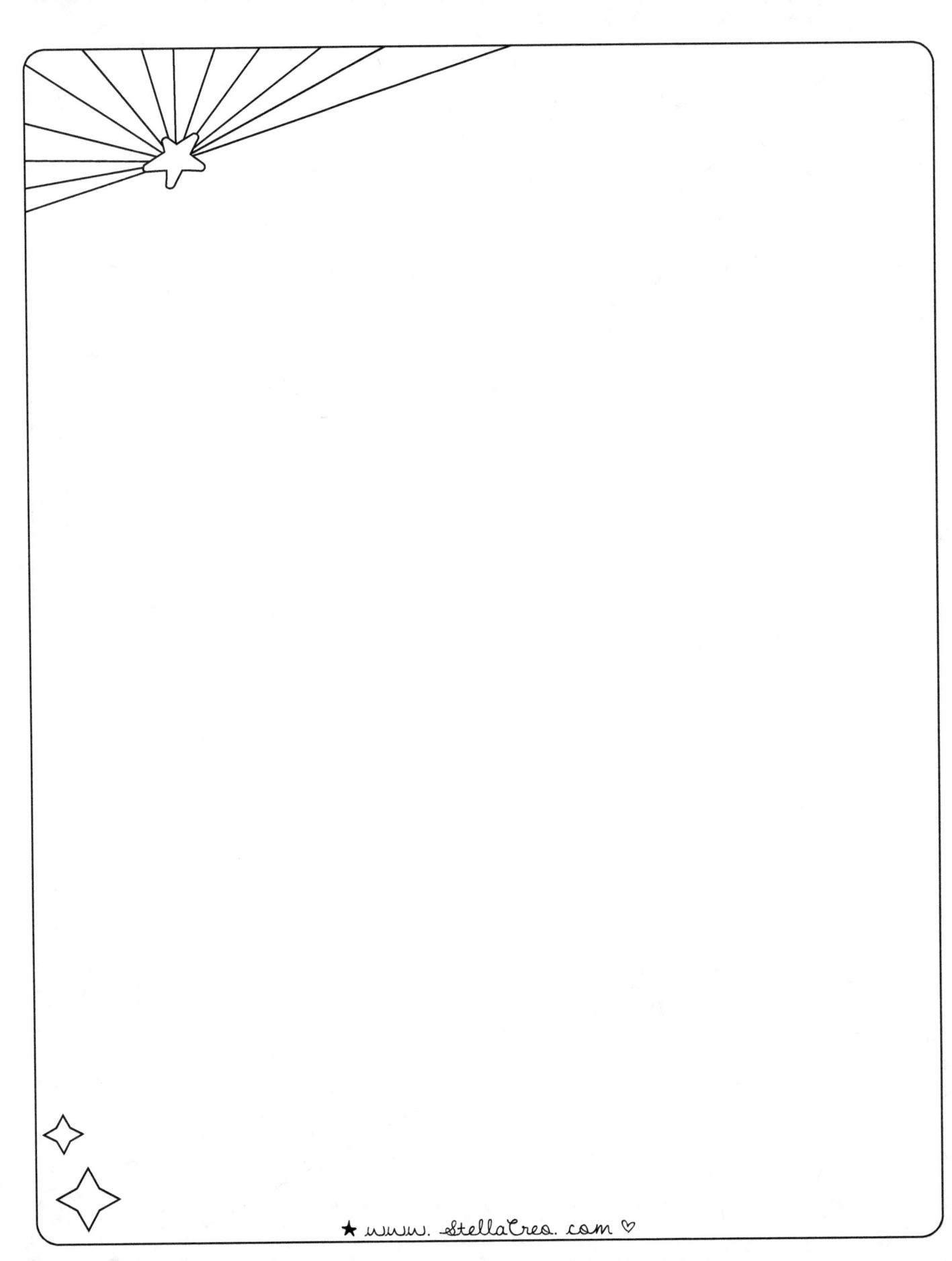

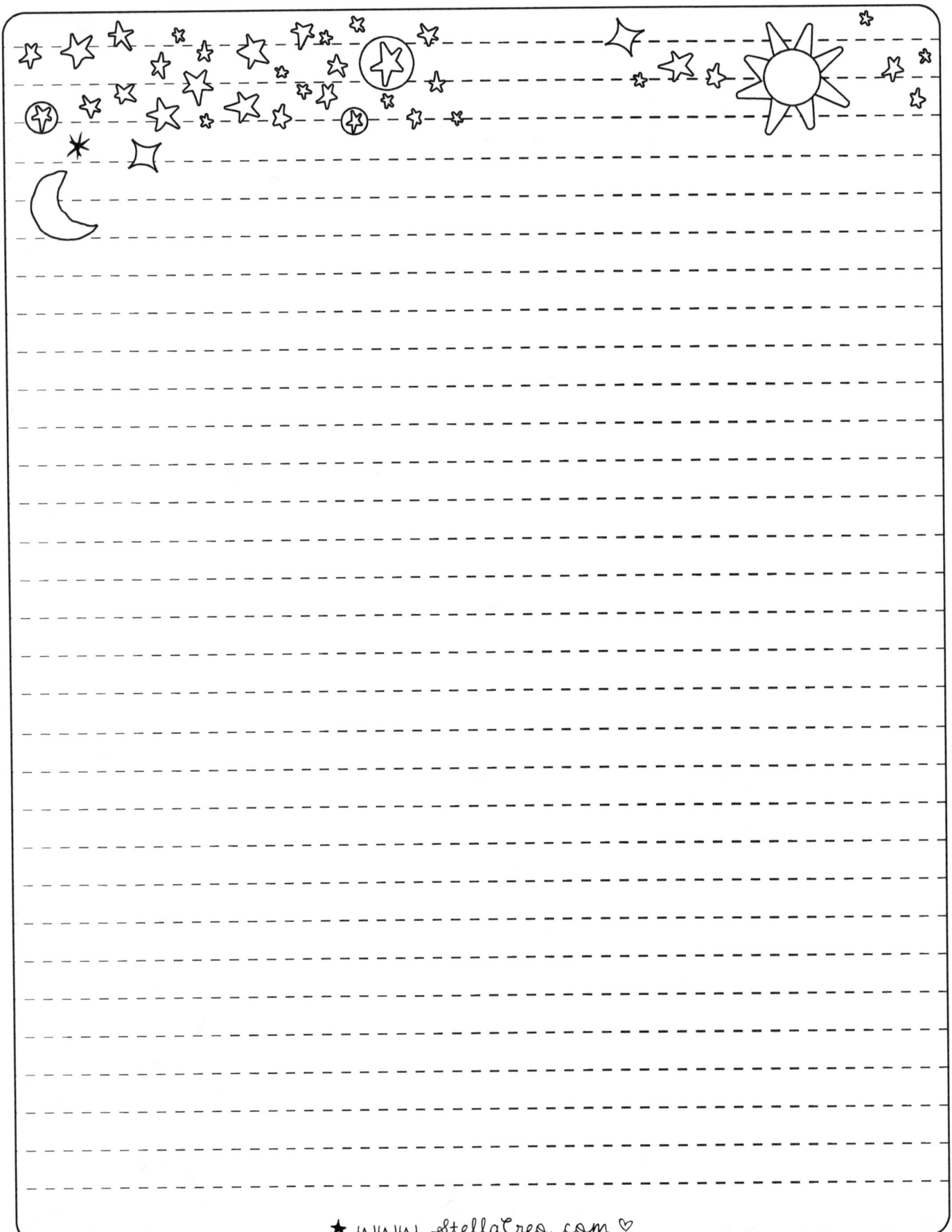

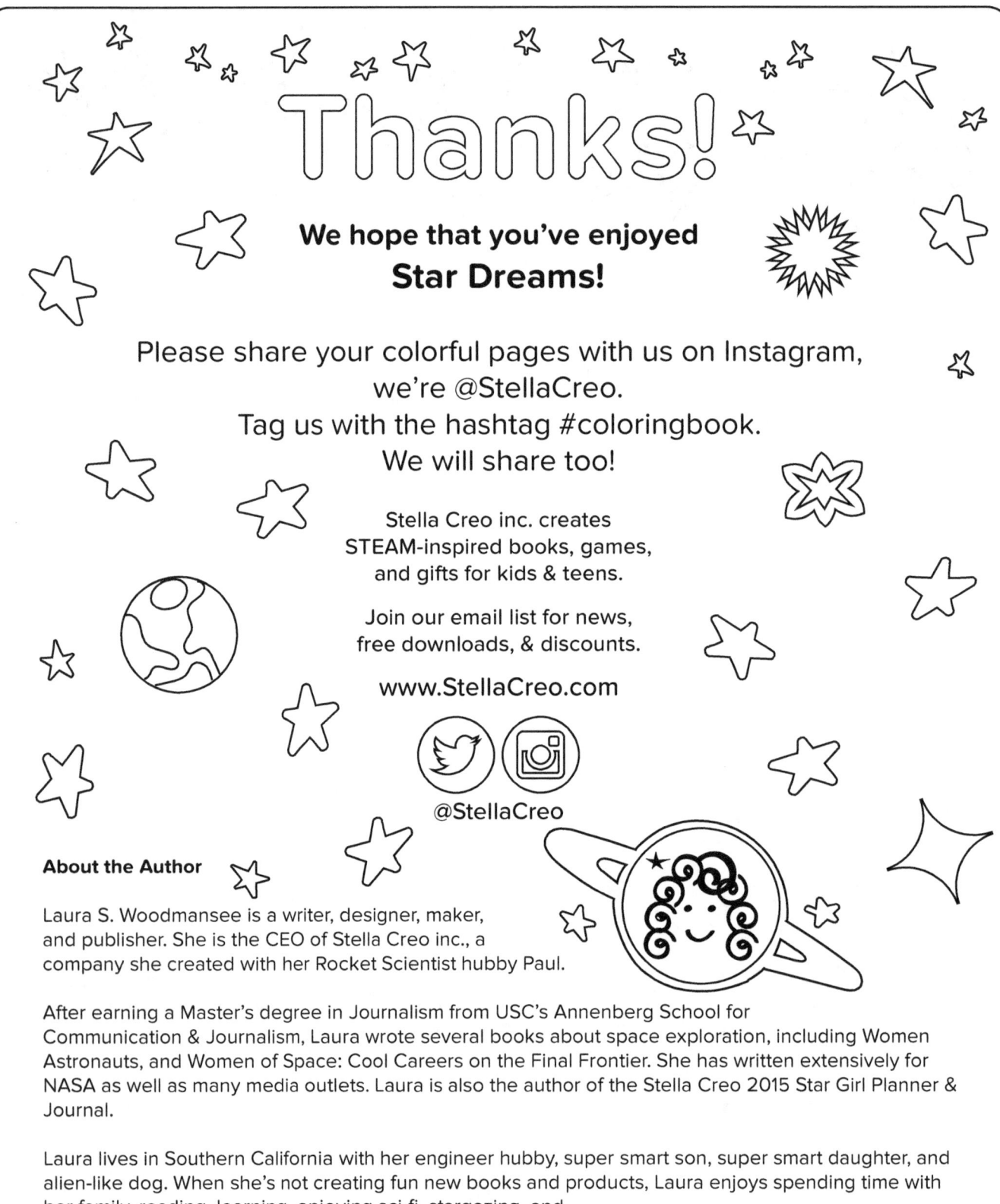

Thanks!

We hope that you've enjoyed
Star Dreams!

Please share your colorful pages with us on Instagram,
we're @StellaCreo.
Tag us with the hashtag #coloringbook.
We will share too!

Stella Creo inc. creates
STEAM-inspired books, games,
and gifts for kids & teens.

Join our email list for news,
free downloads, & discounts.

www.StellaCreo.com

@StellaCreo

About the Author

Laura S. Woodmansee is a writer, designer, maker,
and publisher. She is the CEO of Stella Creo inc., a
company she created with her Rocket Scientist hubby Paul.

After earning a Master's degree in Journalism from USC's Annenberg School for
Communication & Journalism, Laura wrote several books about space exploration, including Women
Astronauts, and Women of Space: Cool Careers on the Final Frontier. She has written extensively for
NASA as well as many media outlets. Laura is also the author of the Stella Creo 2015 Star Girl Planner &
Journal.

Laura lives in Southern California with her engineer hubby, super smart son, super smart daughter, and
alien-like dog. When she's not creating fun new books and products, Laura enjoys spending time with
her family, reading, learning, enjoying sci-fi, stargazing, and
dreaming about what (and who) is out there beyond Earth.
In case you haven't guessed by now, she's a true space geek ;)
Keep in touch with Laura on Twitter and Instagram:
@LauraWoodmansee and @StellaCreo.

★ www. StellaCreo. com ♡